Mother of My Invention

praise for *Mother of My Invention*

When we think of an American Fifties home, we may think of TV shows like *Father Knows Best,* Leave it to Beaver, and *Ozzie and Harriet*, where home life revolves around the kids and Dad's harmless antics. And the Mom is the rock that makes it work, that gives the Fifties such a safe, secure, and stable feeling.

In *Mother of My Invention*, Janice Airhart describes what it was like to grow up amidst this comfortable, if ironclad, social conformity with a mother who is likened to a historical, deadly storm. Eventually, her schizophrenia forces her husband to institutionalize her.

This stigma in the rigidly wholesome and healthy Fifties causes Airhart as a young child severe anxiety and shame that results in humiliating physical and emotional problems that she details with candor. The same unflinching eye is turned on the horrifying, mad-science treatments her mother receives in order to "fix" her. But every return home is more traumatic than the last for the whole family.

Airhart, as an adult, has very little to go on to piece together who her mother was before her mental decline. As she follows up on every clue, she discovers that as a child, when she thought she'd been busy inventing a mother for herself, she'd actually invented a persona for herself: a pretend, "normal" Fifties girl.

This memoir touches every emotion, but it's also an important story that doesn't just educate us on the trauma we can cause by using "crazy" as a witticism; it is also a piece of our collective history that tells the other side of the Golden Era of the 1950s. Most of all, it's a testament to what children can survive.

— Tara Neilson, 2021 Memoir Contest Judge and author of *Raised in Ruins*, a memoir about growing up in the ruins of a remote Alaskan cannery.

Mother of My Invention

A Motherless Daughter Memoir

By Janice Airhart

Minerva Rising Press
Boca Raton

ISBN: 978-1-950811-16-8

Book design by Brooke Schultz

Printed and bound in USA
First Printing November 2022

Published by Minerva Rising Press
17717 Circle Pond Ct
Boca Raton, FL 33496
www.minervarising.com

praise for *Mother of My Invention*

When we think of an American Fifties home, we may think of TV shows like *Father Knows Best,* Leave it to Beaver, and *Ozzie and Harriet*, where home life revolves around the kids and Dad's harmless antics. And the Mom is the rock that makes it work, that gives the Fifties such a safe, secure, and stable feeling.

In *Mother of My Invention*, Janice Airhart describes what it was like to grow up amidst this comfortable, if ironclad, social conformity with a mother who is likened to a historical, deadly storm. Eventually, her schizophrenia forces her husband to institutionalize her.

This stigma in the rigidly wholesome and healthy Fifties causes Airhart as a young child severe anxiety and shame that results in humiliating physical and emotional problems that she details with candor. The same unflinching eye is turned on the horrifying, mad-science treatments her mother receives in order to "fix" her. But every return home is more traumatic than the last for the whole family.

Airhart, as an adult, has very little to go on to piece together who her mother was before her mental decline. As she follows up on every clue, she discovers that as a child, when she thought she'd been busy inventing a mother for herself, she'd actually invented a persona for herself: a pretend, "normal" Fifties girl.

This memoir touches every emotion, but it's also an important story that doesn't just educate us on the trauma we can cause by using "crazy" as a witticism; it is also a piece of our collective history that tells the other side of the Golden Era of the 1950s. Most of all, it's a testament to what children can survive.

— Tara Neilson, 2021 Memoir Contest Judge and author of *Raised in Ruins*, a memoir about growing up in the ruins of a remote Alaskan cannery.

For motherless daughters everywhere.

May you find the mothers you need in those around you.

contents

author's note

A memoir is a product of memory, and no memory records as accurately as a video camera. Neither do two people remember the same aspects of an event. I fully acknowledge that I may have misremembered or misinterpreted incidents or conversations. Nevertheless, I've attempted to faithfully illustrate my search for the mother I lost because of sustained and heritable mental illness and describe what I discovered along the way. In this pursuit, I'm incredibly grateful for surviving hospital records, excerpted here with slight revisions for clarity, and which help tell both my story and my mother's.

Part I

I
Asylum: 2019

"Are you a patient?" asks the woman at the guard shack, "If not, you can't come in." Apparently, an abandoned insane asylum is a magnet for curiosity seekers and ghost hunters.

My husband pleads my case. "We'd just like to drive through. Maybe take some pictures. My wife's mother was a resident here a long time ago." Named the Louisiana Hospital for the Insane when it opened in 1906, the institution now appears on a couple of online haunted places lists.

From the passenger side, I lean forward and look the woman in the eye.

"Don't call attention to yourselves," she says before closing her window.

We make our way around and along the major

roads: Melody Lane, Rainbow Drive, Euclid Street. Some are no longer marked. The dozens of abandoned two-story brick residential halls, which housed over 3000 patients in the 1960s, dot the landscape. Covered walkways once connected many of the halls at the center, radiating from the core like spider legs. Some are set apart, a remnant of the once-segregated complex. Soon the Rose Cottage comes into view, recognizable from the picture I printed from the internet.

"Let's stop here for a minute," I say, and my husband pulls to the side of the road outside the oldest original building on the grounds. The cottage housed a morgue, a laboratory, and electroconvulsive therapy (ECT) equipment during the years my mother was a resident. It seems so small. My family must have driven on this road when visiting her, but the building isn't familiar. I snap several pictures through the open car window.

"Go ahead and get out," my husband urges, "Get closer."

But I'm reluctant to leave the safety of our car, afraid getting out might draw attention. "Drive ahead so I can get a side view." I wonder if my mother came here for treatments or if they brought the ECT equipment to her.

Driving northwest from the entrance, we soon see the dairy barn, which once housed the cattle that provided occupation for residents. The barn and adjacent stables are now in disrepair. Billboards nearby advertise a "Save the Dairy Barn" campaign to keep the structures from deteriorating further.

Both the Rose Cottage and the dairy barn are on the National Register of Historic Places. Maybe my mother visited these places often, or maybe she never did. No one knows now.

When my husband stops the car and gets out, I do too. We're far from the guard shack now, all the way to the edge of the highway—no one's likely to see us here. I take more pictures and look back toward the sprawling hospital grounds, which once spanned 400 acres. The dairy barn is the only building I recognize.

The last time I'd been here was 1965, the summer I was twelve. Our church in Lake Charles hosted a picnic on the lush, rolling hills surrounding the barn. My father, my siblings, and I were vital members of the congregation, and the afternoon outing signified the other members' love for us—all five of us, including my mother, who most had never met. Many of the women present had been like mothers to me, and I was mortified that they now bore witness to that which separated our family from theirs. The other youths and I ran up and down the hill leading to the dairy barn and distant from the grassy expanse of the picnic area. I hoped to draw attention away from the person at the center of the church's intent. The woman who stared at her plate, who took deliberate bites without speaking.

I was tense with fear that my mother's behavior would become violent or bizarre, as I knew too well it could be. To my immense relief, the afternoon passed without incident, and we returned to our motherless home without adding to the stigma I'd arrived with.

I'd always counted on the distance between our home in Lake Charles and the hospital in Pineville, a couple of hours north, to keep the two halves of my life separate, and I was eager to reestablish that distance. I didn't know how to navigate the thin line between my family's reality and our pretense of normalcy.

My mother died a few months after the picnic, and there had been no reason to come back again. Instead, I devoted myself to the discovery of who my mother had been before she lived here. Who was this woman whose life had once been rich with promise but ended too soon in a psychiatric institution, separated from her husband and children? The woman whose life and death and genes determined who I might become? Returning to the site that represented such misery seemed too dangerous. But the sudden, tragic death of a sister-in-law who lived nearby provided an opportunity to acknowledge this institution's place in my history.

"Let's drive back toward the road we came in on," I suggest, "I want a better look at the dormitories." There are several clusters of ramshackle two-story residence halls just inside the main entrance from State Highway 71.

Patches of overgrown weeds, small naturally carved gullies, pools of water from recent rains, and clusters of stories-tall, rail-straight pine trees surround concrete block buildings. The overstory provides a cooling shade and a carpet of pine needles and cones. A basketball goal, missing its net, still stands near the cracked and crumbling road where we stop to inspect the three halls flanking the pavement.

My mother lived—and died—in Ward 54, but that label means nothing today. Buildings were renumbered or renamed and housed hundreds—if not thousands—of other patients after her death. Native vines now cling to the brick exteriors and wind up toward and out of eaves, while shoulder-high brush huddles close to each building's perimeter. Windowpanes are covered in foil or paper artwork. Some are cracked; all are dirty. Another older two-story building sits at the end of the road, with missing windowpanes and shingles. Unlike the others, it's constructed of wood, but random planks of siding are gone. The height of the overgrowth suggests it was abandoned decades earlier than its close neighbors.

I tromp over ankle-high weeds and sidestep puddles to peer inside a few windows. The rooms are small and nearly identical. A closet and built-in storage niche hugs the opposite wall. Linoleum floors are cracked and littered with debris, as though residents rushed out en masse in the middle of the night bearing only what they could carry. A large lobby opens from the front hallway. Nothing I see is familiar. When our family came here, my brother, sister, and I sat in the car while Dad signed our mother out for a day pass and a drive into town.

With slumped shoulders and my forehead resting

against a windowpane, a breath catches in my throat. I wonder how it felt to be confined within these walls, within one of these small rooms. There might have been occasional trips to the sewing cottage or the dairy barn or a stroll on one of the faint trails still visible, but I can't know how often that was possible. I've spent a good portion of my life wondering who my mother was *before* they diagnosed her with schizophrenia, but almost none wondering what life was like for her *after* her diagnosis and during the many years as an unwilling hospital resident. Being here, on the same ground she'd walked when she was allowed that privilege, tightens my chest. My heart aches for the loneliness she must have felt at being separated from everyone and everything she knew. Who was this woman? What did she endure? Regardless of the anger and confusion she must have known when she was admitted, and regardless of the paranoid delusions she was subject to once her brain malfunctioned, complete isolation from the familiar could itself incite madness. These walls had witnessed the heartbreaking misery of countless souls who hid behind them for safety or pounded them in fury—the stories they might tell unbearable to those left behind.

I often wonder where they all are, the children and grandchildren of the certifiably insane. Since my mother's death, I've met no one—*not one person*—whose parent was committed against their will as a long-term resident of such a facility, one of hundreds across the nation. Where are the other children of the residents of Louisiana facilities in the 50s and

60s? There would be thousands. Of course, I've only ever asked the question silently, hypothetically. And almost as soon as I ask it, I know the answer: we don't talk about our nearness to insanity. We know better than to call attention to ourselves.

II
Missing Pieces: 1952

My mother went missing before I was born. It wasn't a physical disappearance ... at first. She disappeared into her own reality in pieces, neuron by neuron. Delusion heaped upon delusion until her thoughts were so fractured they resembled a stranger's. Months before I was born, my father was confused when Barbara Jean, Bobbie, confided her conviction that the neighbors across the street were spying on her and spreading malicious gossip. My parents had played bridge with this couple for years, and they'd sometimes babysat in a pinch for five-year-old Karen and three-year-old Jon. This sudden mistrust of good friends was baffling.

While Bobbie's suspicions were confusing,

Dad grew alarmed when he came home from work to find Jon up to his ears, literally head to toe, in green enamel he'd been applying with gusto to the basement stairs. Bobbie was upstairs reading.

Dad was not only embarrassed, but frightened when a pregnant Bobbie marched into her obstetrician's office and demanded a declaration of love from the doctor. It was clear the beautiful, smart, brown-eyed brunette with the radiant smile, the woman he'd once marveled would consent to marry him, was seriously ill. He wasn't sure where his wife had gone.

A few short months later, when I was still an infant, our family moved from Cincinnati to Lake Charles, Louisiana so my father could assume duties as Chief Chemist at soon-to-open W. R. Grace Chemical Plant. There was a brief stay in Indianapolis for my mother and siblings and me while she received outpatient psychiatric treatment and Dad purchased a home. After the move and a few more months of ineffective psychiatric care in Lake Charles, my mother was judicially committed for the first time, with a tentative diagnosis of paranoid schizophrenia, to Southeastern Louisiana State Hospital in Mandeville, Louisiana, about a four-hour drive from our new home. It was the first of two institutions where she would spend the rest of her life. Her disappearance was now physical as well.

I was less than a year old and presumably resplendent with all the normal, obnoxious infant needs. Who met those needs, I have no idea. There was formula, I assume. Bottles. There would've been sagging wet or poopy cloth diapers, crying in the night when I didn't feel sleepy, throwing up on freshly washed and ironed white Oxford shirts. Who mixed the formula? Who held the bottles? Who ironed the shirts and cleaned up the messes? There's no one left who knows. The closest extended family was nearly a thousand miles away; no relative could provide motherly care or womanly example.

Hired babysitters doubled as housekeepers when we were young; some of them no doubt filled my infant needs. My sister Karen once reminded me of their names, but I've forgotten most, and now Karen's gone. There was a Mrs. Bourgeois and a Mrs. Fruge, both local ladies who presumably brought their traditional Cajun food and Catholic culture into our Yankee Protestant home. I've learned to appreciate the Cajun love of family and zydeco music, Catholic faith observance, and well-seasoned, spicy food. Perhaps the women hired were wives of my father's coworkers, but I'm not sure. All I know is I was suspicious of their care for us, as one of them once washed my face with a pair of my underwear. Karen insisted they must have been clean underwear, but still. I wish I remembered more of these hired women in our home beyond the underwear incident, because their consistent presence would have shaped my early fears and perceptions of the world.

When Karen and my brother Jon were older and I was not yet in school, the sitter I remember best is Mrs. Brown, the wife of an Air Force officer stationed at Chennault Air Force Base in town. She once brought puppies to spend the day with us. Fat little brown furballs with breath that smelled of bologna. They wriggled just out of reach under my bed. At four years old, I would've outgrown bottles and diapers. Mrs. Brown was a large woman and spent a good deal of her time reading magazines while stretched out on the sofa or the bed where the puppies squirmed underneath. Aside from reading magazines and bringing puppies, Mrs. Brown's most memorable contribution to my early education in womanly arts was preparing a snack of mayonnaise spread on white bread. I still love mayonnaise, fat brown puppies, and reading in bed. It could've been worse.

Besides the on again, off again babysitters or housekeepers, we were often in the company of church women like Lois Bekkerus, Mae Hill, and Kathleen Kaufmann. These women provided my deepest impressions of what a woman should be. Our family attended church faithfully, often more than once a week. As a single parent, my father gratefully accepted the motherly attentions of the church women toward his three young children; it may have been his primary lifeline.

Lois had once been a special education teacher. She and her husband had a daughter with disabilities only a few years younger than me. Years later, Lois worked with children at a preschool program my son and daughter attended when they were young, and which eventually expanded to care for children like our nephew Jason, who was born with spina bifida. Lois was a gentle presence throughout my childhood and into the childhoods of my own children. She taught Sunday School classes with patience and dedication, always with a smile and sometimes a wry chuckle. She dispensed wisdom without reproof, often while leaning in for a hug. More than any other woman of my youth, Lois modeled a life of faithful service.

When I was an adolescent, Mae brightened youth events with laughter and stories. Her daughter was a peer of my brother, but because our church congregation was small, youth groups spanned a wide range of ages, usually including one or both of my siblings and myself. Mae sometimes chauffeured the group, and we vied to ride in her car so we could trade jokes and lively conversation while singing our way to outings. Mae's rumble of laughter at the merriment and her obvious joy in our presence was a bonus.

Kathleen was a quieter presence, reserved, yet willing to supervise youth activities when her children joined them. She often volunteered to prepare or serve a meal, or perhaps mop the floor or clean the windows, along with her sometimes cantankerous husband. Kathleen taught me that no task which strengthened the community was beneath her, that acts of service are their own reward.

After a church service, or after we returned from the skating rink or the swimming pool, the church women and their children returned to their respective homes. My siblings and I returned to our comfortable but quiet house without a mother. I was confident Lois, Mae, and Kathleen accepted us—loved us, even—but the fact remained that none of them was my mother.

After years of observing the women around me—teachers, mothers of friends, and neighbors—I began to understand the depth of loss I was dealing with. I hadn't yet learned the myriad ways to lose someone. I have friends who've lost a parent to cancer or heart disease. My coworker Melinda lost her grandmother to Alzheimer's. My good friend Carolyn lost a teenaged son to suicide. Divorced parents are notorious for becoming lost, as are parents who give up children for adoption. How or why someone is lost is a puzzle, but losing someone is not like the daily crossword, where the solution comes in tomorrow's newspaper. Sometimes the clues don't make sense and the words don't fit. Sometimes it's pointless to ask how or why someone is missing. The dilemma is how to move forward, how to pick up what pieces are left and make do without the ones you lost; the real puzzle is not knowing what pieces are missing. There's no box top with a cover photo, and you don't know what image you're creating.

In 2005, I obtained my mother's hospital records from her four earliest institutional years, still the most exhaustive information I have. I've scoured them for clues, but I can't know which notes represent my mother's true self. Which piece is the missing one that explains who she might've been or who I'd become as the daughter of a psychotic woman?

Before I learned to keep my keys in that certain pocket of my purse whenever they weren't in the car's ignition, I used to search for lost keys. I've had my husband call my missing cell phone. I once bought the perfect Christmas gift for my son and then lost it. I opened every drawer in every dresser in the house, searched every corner of the closet I knew I'd hid it in, and looked inside the plastic bins of Christmas wrap under the bed. No luck. But tucked away in other drawers, I found old journals, a couple of unfinished novel manuscripts, photo albums, and travel diaries from places I've been: London, New York, Rome, Pompeii, Guyana. Places that helped me see the world through fresh eyes.

In searching for my mother, I uncovered puzzle pieces of unexpected shapes and sizes, each changing the shape of the void I sought to fill. I analyzed people and relationships and considered experiences that pruned deadwood or encouraged growth—often both.

That's the unexpected joy of what you find when you're looking for something else. You start out thinking you have to find the mother you lost in order to know who you are—or maybe just to assure yourself you won't end up as she did. You can't find the missing pieces until you've searched and come up empty, though. First, you must know something you should've had has gone missing.

Southeast Louisiana Hospital
Henke, Barbara
Hospital Number 201
May 25, 1953

Admission Notes

The patient is a judicial commitment from Calcasieu Parish. She is a white female, thirty years of age, and lives in Lake Charles, Louisiana. The husband was the informant.

The patient has shown signs of mental illness since approximately October 15, 1952. Her symptoms began following the birth of the third of her children, who is now ten months old. Her last baby was born with a birthmark. She began to worry and develop ideas about her husband's fidelity. She wanted to leave her husband and wanted to stage a party at which she intended to announce her impending divorce. She decided at that time that she was in love with someone else, although she was very confused. She began to misinterpret and attach special significance to very odd occurrences and developed widespread ideas of reference, believing people were talking about her.

She was admitted into Norway Foundation Hospital at Indianapolis, Indiana, and was treated with insulin. She was diagnosed with depression, illusions, and misinterpretation.

She rejoined her husband and was brought to Lake Charles. She appeared to be all right for a while following discharge from the hospital; but on coming to Lake Charles, approximately two months ago, she began to get nervous, irritable, and jumpy. She received a few ESTs [electroshock treatments] at this time, the exact number not being known by the informant. She then seemed all good for a while, but she was followed in psychotherapy by Dr. Funk of Lake Charles. The husband said that she and Dr. Funk did not hit it off very well, and Dr. Funk stated he could not get the patient to focus on her problems. He apparently felt that her problems largely lay in the sexual area.

III

The Storm: 1957

They refused to give in to what was coming. "Seen this kind before. Nothing but a little storm," said the shopkeepers and fishermen of Cameron Parish, Louisiana, in the summer of 1957. "No need to go running up the coast yet," said fathers and grandfathers to anxious wives and children, "We'll see, come tomorrow."

During the night, wind shrieked through gaps under doors and windows. Rain pelted tin roofs, and rising water lapped at cement block foundations. Soon it was too late to go—the road was washed out.

When Hurricane Audrey slammed into the south Louisiana coast in the predawn hours of June 27, the storm surge topped telephone poles, and water moccasins plunged inland with the tide. While I remember the drama of the hurricane and its impact, my memory of details is spotty—I was not yet five years old. Some things I was told by others; some things I didn't learn until many years later, from historical accounts. Regardless, it's my first cohesive memory of life's events, and an intensely dramatic one at that.

Audrey sucked entire communities into her watery arms, then dumped them: masses of tangled brush, people, and snakes; livestock, stoves, and quilts; shoes, rafters, and more. Nothing stood intact in the coastal town of Cameron but the courthouse. Nearly five hundred were dead.

In 1957, my family and I were weathering our own kind of storm. Dad, Jon, Karen, and I lived about fifty miles inland from the Gulf of Mexico in Lake Charles. Since 1953, my mother had been in and out of psychiatric facilities in two states and four cities before being diagnosed with schizophrenia, and the collateral damage hadn't been fully assessed. There was a disconnect between who she'd been and who the disease made her. She'd been gone so long, I barely remembered her.

My father was a prolific photographer, yet I only have a handful of pictures of my mother, some of which represent stories I've invented for myself. My favorite is one my father took in 1944, before their marriage. Mother's standing at the bottom of snow-covered steps at Douglass College for Women in a fur coat and black boots, with a notebook in her left arm. A cigarette dangles from her right hand, barely visible against the backdrop of snow. She's beaming up at my father, poised to place one boot on the next step. I see a pretty woman with dancing eyes and faintly familiar features who pauses for a black-and-white remembrance. "Hurry, Fred," she seems to say, "We have a wonderful future to get to."

Eight years into that future, there's another photo. She's lying across her bed and I'm lying facedown along the length of her chest, heart to heart. My infant head is raised as I look toward the camera my father holds. My left hand clutches the silk scarf tied at my mother's throat, and her fingertips rest lightly against my side. I can see the side of her face in the picture, but I can't tell if she sees me or not.

Mother's behavior had been growing more bizarre. What Dad couldn't ignore was her conviction that he was trying to kill her, and the housekeeper hired to help was trying to turn her children against her. Violent outbursts and angry attempts to defend against perceived danger grew more pronounced. My brother and sister suffered inattention and occasional dangerous episodes that remain mostly forgotten. Karen's health suffered as well, and to what extent her asthma and potentially fatal allergic reactions were physiological rather than emotional responses to those episodes is unclear. The inhaler she carried with her until the end of her life and the daily injections administered behind the locked bathroom door throughout her youth calmed her skin rashes, tracheal constriction, and respiratory inflammation, but eventually eroded her health. Even in 1957, it seemed safer for all of us if Mother lived somewhere else.

Somewhere else was Southeast Louisiana State Hospital in Mandeville, across Lake Pontchartrain from New Orleans. When Dad obtained commitment papers, authorized by the sheriff and Calcasieu Parish Coroner, he was twenty-nine and Mother was thirty. Karen, Jon, and I were five, three, and ten months. During the next four years, my mother was subjected to every cutting-edge schizophrenia cure known to psychiatry in the 50s: warm or bracingly cold-water baths, drug-induced comas, electric shocks, and tranquilizers. All were designed to calm unwanted thoughts and erratic behavior; they had no effect on the course of the disease itself.

In May 1957, after four years of hospitalization, Mother's doctor acknowledged she would "be a chronic hospital problem for some time," and recommended she be transferred to another state psychiatric hospital in Pineville, closer to Lake Charles. Dad collected my mother from Mandeville and drove her to Central State Hospital on May 18th. Hurricane Audrey hit six weeks later.

Audrey developed more rapidly than most hurricanes. She'd been brewing only a couple of days over the Bay of Campeche in the Gulf of Mexico, and communications weren't reliable in the fishing communities along the coast. Weather radar was available, but most estimates predicted Audrey would hit further west along the east Texas coast, about twenty-four hours later than she did. A lot of wait-and-see folks were trapped.

Meanwhile, Lake Charles was buzzing. "Where do ya' think she'll hit? You gonna stick around?" Dad took us to the A&P to stock up on canned food and milk, and it seemed everyone else in town—those who hadn't moved further inland—did the same. Lines were long, and while they waited, people traded tips on riding out a hurricane. "You got to crack a window on the side opposite the wind," or "Stay in a room without bare windows so glass won't fly at you."

When we got home, Dad nailed plywood over the front picture window, the single large pane in our living room, and heaved a mattress up against the glass inside to shield us in case broken shards took flight. We stashed outdoor toys and chairs in the garage.

I could barely sleep that night, shivery all over with anticipation. I lay on my back and peeked up through the crisscrossed wire frame at the bottom of the bunk bed I shared with Karen. I'd squeeze my eyes shut tight, then I'd hear the wind howling or light snoring in the bed above, and they'd pop open again until exhaustion bested me.

The coast got hit about four o'clock in the morning, while those who could, slept. They woke to rising water in the towns of Cameron, Creole, and Grand Chenier. Their frame houses were built on stilts, blocks, or piers, high off the ground to protect against flooding, but stilts snapped like toothpicks against hurricane-force wind and twelve-foot storm surge. Nothing like Audrey had ever crossed their coast before.

A hurricane spirals counterclockwise, first bringing winds from the east to pound whatever faces east or north. Then comes the hurricane's eye, surrounded by walls of rain, and followed by westerly winds to batter everything facing the west or south. The eye of a moderate-sized hurricane is thirty miles or more across. If it's moving only ten miles an hour, it can take three hours for the eye to pass.

When the eye of a hurricane stalls over you, you can get fooled into thinking the worst is over. The sheets of driving rain stop, and the sky clears, so the sun blazes as strong as it does on other summer days in Louisiana, but the silence is as sudden as a thunderclap. It's fascinating, that switch from furious squalling to abrupt, bright calm, akin to the sudden calm we'd experienced when Mother moved from our home to the hospital. Audrey's eye lured Dad outside.

"Stay here," Dad unlatched the screen door and stepped out into the quiet of the hurricane's eye and waited for what came next. Jon, Karen, and I stared through the screen as he assessed the surrounding threat. He stood for a good while, watching. I'm not sure what he was thinking, but maybe he was just drinking in the calm. In pictures I've seen since, roof shingles dotted the yards on our block and water crept up to porch steps. We assumed the debris in our backyard was what our home had sacrificed to Audrey's turbulent winds.

When the wind picked up again, Dad came inside, latched the screen, and locked the back door. By then, the power was off, and we spent the second half of the storm in our plywood-shuttered living room. Dad read to us from *A Child's Garden of Verses* in the glow of the Coleman lantern we used for camping trips while the wind had its turn at the other side of the house. We ate crackers, cheese, and potted meat with our fingers, as though we were on an impromptu camping trip indoors. I burrowed down in the warmth of the white shaggy rug that covered the oak floor of our living room throughout my childhood, content to be surrounded by the people I loved most and smug with the sense that I had all I'd ever need. I was unaware of the losses around me.

We didn't know yet how many roofs in our neighborhood were stripped. None of us was aware of the lives lost to our south. I didn't learn until years later how the boats streamed up the ship channel into Lake Charles bearing Cameron's dead, and bus after bus rolled into town with survivors, beaten by splintered wood, half-drowned, and snake bitten. I didn't know about the mass grave they dug behind Sacred Heart of Jesus Catholic Church in Creole or the piles of cattle carcasses they burned along the beach to control the stench.

More recent hurricanes like Katrina, Rita, and Laura proved as damaging, if not as deadly, but during the last half of the twentieth century, when someone mentioned "the storm," longtime residents of Cameron and Creole knew exactly which storm you meant. They'd likely tell you a story about how they survived Audrey, about who and what they lost.

Not me. My heart is likely to race a little with

subdued excitement. I might stifle a smile, guilty for remembering with pleasure what pains so many others. I'm tempted to say my heart ached for a mother's arms to hold me during the harrowing hours of a deadly storm, but I won't—it was a while before I knew that hunger. In 1957, my world was only large enough for the four Henkes who sheltered through the night and shared cold Vienna sausages on paper plates in our darkened living room on Eighteenth Street. How could I know what I was missing?

During my mother's occasional weekend passes home in the years previous, my sister said there were tempestuous arguments and angry accusations. I wish I knew how I reacted to the chaos, but I don't. Perhaps I hid behind furniture or in the large closet of the room my sister and I once shared, beneath the row of hanging dresses and such. I remember it as safe and welcoming. Maybe I'm blocking out pain or confusion over a mother who didn't cuddle or whisper sweet words into my ear. Who didn't laugh and play patty-cake or "this little piggy" as I did with my own children. Who didn't teach me how mothers imprint their essence on their daughters. Until I witnessed these small acts demonstrated by other mothers, I didn't know my heart would someday yearn for them with such intense sorrow. I didn't understand the burden of shame that loss would carry, not until I entered the public arena of elementary school and observed other families. All I knew was my father and siblings loved me, and that was sufficient.

We didn't know that we were living in the storm's eye until the year after Audrey hit, when my mother was discharged from the hospital to live with us for ten months. It was then that our own family storm raged, and it became clear Barbara Jean's former personality had been erased by a combination of her disease and the treatments for it. There was no hope of reclaiming the mother I might have had, and my siblings and I learned to disappear during the alternate rages and electroshock-induced stupors which characterized those months. Hurricane Audrey didn't prepare me for this kind of assault on my emotions. Instead, Audrey had sung a mother's lullaby for me—albeit a lively one—with her rushing winds and driving rains, while I snuggled into the safety of my family's warm regard. I was almost loath for our enforced dormancy to end, but storms have a way of forcing us to face the aftermath; there's no hiding from their truths.

When the storm winds calmed, Dad unlatched the doors and pulled the plywood from the windows. We spilled outside to survey the flooded streets and Karen remembered Jon floating a toy boat down the new river in our front yard. Until electricity was restored, we offered the use of our gas-powered refrigerator to the Lanier family on the west side of us and to the Rushtons on the east.

Dad pulled his ladder out of the garage and crawled up to the roof. We'd lost only part of one shingle. None of the lost shingles scattered across our section of the block were ours at all. Most belonged to the Laniers, whose roof was mottled with bare spaces.

Dad never got over that in nearly forty years of telling and retelling. "We only lost part of a shingle," he'd say, "We're so lucky we didn't lose any more."

Southeast Louisiana Hospital
Henke, Barbara
Hospital Number 201
May 25, 1953

Admission Notes:

At the time of admission, the patient was oriented as to time and place but seemed confused and spoke in an irrelevant fashion with much tangential association. She had one or two clang associations and was hostile towards being admitted but seemed somewhat reassured by the physician. The tentative diagnosis was schizophrenic reaction, paranoid type.

Mental State:

This is a thirty-year-old housewife who appears disheveled and untidy at times, occasionally affecting bizarre dress. Her symptoms include marked confusion, disorientation, and disorganization. She shows a mild degree of excitement with a variability of her affective responses and apparent inconstancy of moods not appropriate to occurrences in the external environment. The thought content is predominated by the confusion and disorganization present but shows a suggestion of widespread delusional ideas of persecution and somatic delusions. Her sensorium is cloudy, and she was unable to cooperate with formal testing, so an evaluation of her intellectual functioning was not possible.

Physical Examination:

This thirty-year-old, married, white female was unable to cooperate for the system review and past history, but the informant gave no history of serious illness. Presently the patient complains of some menstrual flooding since the birth of her last baby ten months ago. Physical examination revealed an essentially healthy, young, adult woman.

IV
Everything's Fine Here

Could I *catch* schizophrenia? Could living in the same house with a schizophrenic mother make me crazy too? Would I be just like her someday? These questions tormented me throughout childhood, but because I was afraid to know the answers, I never asked them. Intentional or not, Dad made room for my fears by separating us from Mother, "for our protection." Anxiety prompted vigilance in guarding my fragile self-image. *I will not go crazy.*

It's a lot harder to convince people you're not crazy than you might think. Humans try to fit into cultural norms to avoid being ostracized, but learning acceptable ways to respond to what's expected is exhausting, especially when consequences are the primary teacher. Convincing *yourself* you're not crazy is challenging too. In the 1950s, having a mother who was not only schizophrenic but committed to the state insane asylum guaranteed I was extraordinary, and not in a good way. The only logical response was to pretend everything was fine.

Pretending was easy enough while my mother lived so far away, and I could mimic behaviors as if I were just like every other neighborhood girl. I giggled at the same jokes about nutcases and looney bins but avoided talk of family goings-on. What happened at my house was inconsequential, after all. Why should I care there was no one waiting at home after school except the hired babysitter? I had no clue—except in my imagination—how a mother might welcome her daughter home from school with a hug or a plate of snickerdoodles. Aside from a few close friends, I didn't invite classmates over and didn't enjoy any birthday parties, cakes, or cookies.

"We children of schizophrenics are the great secret keepers, the ones who don't want you to think that anything is wrong," according to Mira Bartók in her memoir, *The Memory Castle.* I would agree but go further. The pretense of normalcy is driven by fear of being overtaken by the disease, of crazy rubbing off and staining your skin like ink from a leaky fountain pen. When I sensed people thought schizophrenia was contagious—and I was a carrier—I made a point to appear sane at all times, whatever the cost. It ended up costing me a sense of identity apart from a disease I might yet fall victim to. Fear is more contagious than the object of fear itself.

In the 1950s, a prevailing psychological theory about the "schizophrenogenic mother" suggested the child's mother caused schizophrenia. This wasn't the first, and sadly, it won't be the last time we blame women for social ills, even ones that befall mostly women—maybe *especially* those. During the last half of the nineteenth century, hordes of women were committed to psychiatric hospitals by husbands out of convenience. The solution for a wife deemed lazy, hysterical, or too free-minded was to dispose of her by having her declared insane and institutionalized. While this practice was denounced in the twentieth century, the fault of mental illness was, and still is, often laid at the feet of those who suffer from it.

Psychiatrist Frieda Fromm-Reichmann proposed the schizophrenogenic mother concept in 1948, that some mothers—probably ill themselves—literally drove their children crazy by their behavior. Fromm-Reichmann suggested that the mother didn't care properly for the child because of her own delusions and alternated between overprotectiveness and rejection. Schizophrenic tendencies developed as a defense mechanism. To complicate an already complex disease, few effective psychotropic drugs were available. The best approach for protecting the children was to separate them from their sick mothers. This is the strategy my father employed. Maybe *he* thought schizophrenia was contagious, too.

Since my mother's youngest sister, Mary, was also diagnosed with schizophrenia, Fromm-Reichmann's theory seemed confirmed. It must have been heartbreaking for my grandmother, whom I never knew well, to be the scapegoat. In contrast to their older daughter's institutionalization, she and my grandfather had their younger daughter undergo a partial frontal lobotomy, rendering her more dependent on them. While it diminished my aunt's erratic and violent behavior and allowed her to care for her children to some degree, it came with its own set of complications. I only saw my grandparents twice, in brief visits to their New Jersey home when I was five and again when I was twelve. I wonder how they viewed the circumstance that left two of their four children—half—diagnosed with schizophrenia.

Describing a similar pattern, Robert Kolker, in his 2020 book *Hidden Valley Road*, traces one family in which six of their twelve children develop mental illnesses as young adults. It's clear this family, and mine, were hit hard by a familial heritage of mental illness. However, genetic predisposition wasn't well understood in the 50s. In fact, DNA's structure and its role in heredity remained a mystery until the year after my birth and the year of my mother's commitment (1953) when James Watson and Francis Crick deduced from existing evidence that the DNA molecule is a double helix. Their conclusion allowed for more extensive research and understanding of genetic disorders over the next couple of decades. Meanwhile, blame was placed on the easiest target: the mother.

Given the wide acceptance of the schizophrenogenic mother theory in 1953 and the fact that our mother and aunt suffered the same disease, the metamessage for my sister, brother, and me was clear. If Dad were careless enough to allow us in our mother's presence too long, her craziness might infect us too.

The wrongheadedness of this parental blame model didn't gain traction until the 1970s, several years after my mother's death. It might have provided some comfort for my grandmother, but the damage had been done. She didn't die until the 80s after she and my grandfather had helped raise three of their grandchildren and endured Aunt Mary's intermittent periods of catatonia, aggressive scratching and hair-pulling, and occasionally setting fire to the house, stories I didn't hear until I was in my fifties.

My mother had also been a victim of separation from everything familiar after marrying my father. They lived first in Indiana and then Ohio during their early marriage. Our family moved from my birthplace in Cincinnati to Lake Charles shortly after my mother's diagnosis, thousands of miles away from her family in New Jersey. Perhaps this separation was deliberate on my father's part. Just as we were separated from our mother, the schizophrenic, perhaps he orchestrated her separation from her schizophrenogenic mother. Maybe an occasional visit with Mother at the hospital was deemed acceptable exposure. Those visits showed me what crazy looked like: disheveled women rocking plastic baby dolls on the front porch of their dormitories and staring vacantly into the distance and residents shuffling across the lawn while muttering to themselves.

These images helped me create my own carefully crafted noncrazy persona.

In my childhood, we'd pile into the car with anxious dread, silently wait for Dad to check our mother out for the day and head into town for a drive, while my mother sat in a catatonic daze in the front seat. We three kids jabbered and jittered nervously in the back seat.

"On one of our early visits," my brother Jon recalls, "she wasn't talking, and neither was Dad, so I tried to lighten the mood by singing. I sang a couple of verses, getting pretty loud with nobody saying anything, when she suddenly turned around and slapped me across the face ... hard." Jon was about ten, and I was seven. "Well, that stopped my singing and hurt my feelings more than anything. From then on, I was careful to not initiate conversation on those visits, and it caused me to hate them."

Though we dreaded these occasional visits to the hospital, we didn't rebel. Instinct and respect for our father silenced our protest. While Dad had separated us, he clearly found it important that we maintain a relationship with our mother. Maybe he longed for the woman he'd married, or maybe he simply wanted to ensure she was being treated well. Perhaps she begged to see us, or perhaps Dad hoped seeing us would shift something wonky in her brain. Did he still love her? I can't know, but I believe he continued to hope for her recovery.

Tense with the uncertainty about our mother's behavior, we tolerated visits to Pineville for an afternoon every few months so we could return to our *actual* lives a hundred miles away. Our outings often ended with ice cream, perhaps a reward for enduring the inevitable discomfort and negating the unpleasant with the pleasant. The implicit family pact was that we *never* spoke to each other about our mother outside of these visits, much less to anyone else. *Everything's okay with us. Really.*

Experience taught me to keep such details about my home life out of schoolroom conversations. A few empathetic moms and some of my teachers must have known the truth, and God bless them for treating me with compassion. Nothing was ever spoken about my lack of a mother, but it was an obvious fact, and I was convinced *everyone* knew. That no one mentioned it taught me it wasn't an appropriate subject for conversation.

In 1957, the year I turned five, and the same year Hurricane Audrey blustered her way up the Gulf of Mexico, Thorazine changed the lives of mental patients everywhere. It replaced electroshock therapy for many, and at first, my mother's behavior seemed controlled enough that they released her to come home from the hospital.

That's when I first experienced the implications of Mother's illness, when I first understood we weren't a typical family, when I first experienced the tightened chest and knotted stomach at a stray comment about lunatics and funny farms. When vomiting and diarrhea became symptoms of anxiety.

I met classmates' mothers at school, women who spoke endearments to their children and whom I studied with focused intent. My mother alternated between catatonia and wild accusations against my father. She hid things, poorly, from family members or housekeepers. When I inadvertently dumped too much salt on a plate of eggs she'd cooked for me, she ordered me to eat them. Other mothers made cookies for their families; other mothers read bedtime stories. My mother kept the lights on all night as punishment for making noise.

While my older brother and sister took refuge out of the house and roamed the neighborhood with friends, I withdrew into self-selected solitary calm. "If we didn't know where you were," my sister Karen once told me, "We just started looking in corners or behind the furniture. You could be sneaky quiet, reading your picture books." And why not? Books never pass judgement or erupt into violence from unseen provocation. The stories I read and the stories I told myself distanced me from the chaos and deranged threats. A few months later, when the mothers I'd studied with such fascination were confronted with Mother's illness firsthand, some didn't allow their children to play with me.

This, too, became an indelible lesson on the need to pretend everything's fine.

Southeast Louisiana Hospital
Henke, Barbara
Hospital Number 201
April 25, 1954

Course in the Hospital:

This patient was admitted to the semi-open ward and in spite of her rather marked disorganization, was able to cooperate with the ward routine fairly well. After her first week she began to show some increasing excitement and on one occasion slapped another patient and after became assaultive towards one of her attendants. It was necessary for her to be transferred to the closed ward where she was able to adapt better. Her excitement showed exacerbations, and on July 4, 1953 electroconvulsive treatments were ordered. Between July 6, 1953 and August 21, 1953, she received a total of twenty-one electroconvulsive treatments and showed some improvement to these but relapsed almost immediately afterward. On August 27, 1953, Insulin coma treatment was instituted. She received a total of sixty insulin treatments between the time of institution of treatment in August until November 20, 1953. During this time, she had fifty-one comas and for the most part, her response to insulin was uneventful. Her husband remained attentive, frequently visited the patient in spite of her long distance from their home and frequently sought consultations with me. Since she showed no further improvement after insulin coma, we began to discuss the possibility that he might make some arrangement at home to have someone stay with the children and see if it might be possible for her to stay at home with him. He tried taking her home for weekly passes during the months of December and January, and the patient seemed somewhat improved in that she became anxious about her children and inquired about her husband frequently. On April 25, 1954, the patient was placed on Convalescent Status, with the arrangement that she would have a housekeeper in their home and as little stress as possible while she remained there.

V
A Disease Without Cure

According to the National Institutes of Mental Health, the current prevalence of schizophrenia in the US is between 0.25 percent and 0.64 percent. These rates represent more than one million Americans. The National Alliance on Mental Illness reports that twenty percent of American adults suffer from some form of mental illness—more than fifty million. Clinicians agree most estimates under-represent reality because many sufferers are reluctant to report their illness. However, if you know at least a couple hundred people, the chances are good you know a schizophrenic. And if you know someone in their late teens or twenties who committed suicide, they may well have been schizophrenic too. Close to five percent of schizophrenics end their lives by suicide. It's a cruel disease without a cure.

While treatment of schizophrenia has become more effective in the last fifty years, there's still much unknown about causation and some controversy over classifications. It's clear there's a genetic component to the disease, and DNA studies have confirmed sequences that make some individuals more susceptible than others. Why it's "switched on" in some and not others is unclear, but hormonal changes may flip the switch. It most often develops in young men in their late teens and young women in their twenties, when testosterone or estrogen levels surge.

While my mother exhibited symptoms of postpartum depression after the birth of my brother three years earlier, her symptoms either resolved or went underground. It wasn't until her third pregnancy, with me, that her symptoms became alarming. Postpartum depression is a common diagnosis, with an incidence of seven to ten percent in postnatal women, and would've been recognized. Even more serious is postpartum psychosis, a rare condition, which includes symptoms like schizophrenia. In the *Diagnostic and Statistical Manual of Mental Disorders (DSM-5)*, it's listed as one of several "short psychotic disorders" in the schizophrenia spectrum. It's considered short because it resolves within a year or two postpartum, assuming effective treatment. My mother received the recommended treatments for postpartum psychosis, plus some, yet her condition did not resolve before her life ended some thirteen years later. While origins of both psychoses may be similar, resolution is not; it's doubtful they misdiagnosed my mother, though the distinction may simply be a semantics issue. Aside from hormone fluctuations, there are other potential explanations for the origins of schizophrenia, which add to our understanding of both cause and treatment.

Recent studies in epigenetics—neuroepigenetics—have investigated the permanent changes to DNA that result from attachment of methyl groups to the DNA molecule and turn certain genes off or on. Research suggests that this mechanism may account for the environmental factors involved in development of schizophrenia in those who are genetically predisposed. There's also some evidence that attachments of methyl compounds, a process called DNA methylation, may be passed on from a mother to her children, though they aren't certain whether the changes in DNA replication during pregnancy are permanent. What's certain is that schizophrenia is a complex condition, which may encompass a range of causes and therefore exhibit a wide range of symptoms.

Some psychiatrists believe there are specific types of schizophrenia while others believe categorization isn't necessary since treatments are similar. This is the current attitude of the DSM-5, which doesn't use subtypes in schizophrenia descriptions. "Schizophrenia is a severe and chronic mental disorder characterized by disturbances in thought, perception and behavior," is a brief definition, but the DSM-5 includes an extensive list of symptoms. It's characterized by thoughts and images, some auditory and some visual, that appear absolutely real to patients but aren't. Because of these disordered thoughts, disorganized speech often results. Delusions or hallucinations can convince schizophrenics they are personalities ranging everywhere from God to mass murderers; paranoia can convince them that others are trying to harm them. While schizophrenics are capable of violent crimes, they're less likely to murder someone than a sane individual, statistically. My mother was subject to violent outbursts, but it never resulted in serious physical harm.

Elyn R. Saks, a professor of both law and psychiatry, is also successfully controlled by medication to treat her schizophrenia symptoms. In *The Center Cannot Hold: My Journey Through Madness,* published in 2007, Saks claims stress or sudden changes in the environment may trigger psychotic events. She's among the lucky; only about twenty percent of schizophrenics can manage independent living, and the outcome depends on drug effectiveness. Patients respond to antipsychotic medication individually, depending on their unique biochemistry. For Saks, whose primary professional interest is advocacy of fair mental health law, the disease ebbs and flows and is managed by a combination of antipsychotic drugs and psychoanalytic procedures such as talk therapy.

In 1952, the year my mother's symptoms began, talk therapy was fairly crude, and there were no antipsychotic drugs available. That same year, Henri Laborit discovered that high doses of a specific antihistamine (chlorpromazine; trade name Thorazine) changed the mental states of patients emerging from effects of anesthesia after surgery. The calming effects of the drug were dramatic, and mental health professionals took note. The rate of hospitalizations in mental institutions had doubled from the early to the mid-twentieth century, and psychiatry was desperate for alternatives. Practitioners had few tools to work with, aside from electroshock and insulin shock, which did nothing more than dull patients temporarily in between violent or paranoid episodes.

In 1954, the US FDA approved chlorpromazine. By 1964, fifty million people around the world had taken the drug. Despite troubling side effects, it was the first major victory of pharmacological science against mental illness. Chlorpromazine is a safe and effective treatment for a variety of disorders, including bipolar disorder, severe nausea, schizophrenia, and ADHD. It's so widely prescribed and useful historically that it appears on the World Health Organization's List of Essential Medicines. While my mother did receive chlorpromazine, barbiturates were prescribed more frequently for the seizures that resulted from her electroshock therapy.

Before antipsychotic drugs were in widespread use, the most effective treatments were those that shocked the brain into a sort of reset, something like defibrillation does for the heart. The two most often used variations were electroshock and insulin shock, but hydrotherapy could also be effective short term.

Hydrotherapy, immersing the body in first warm and then cold water or exposing the body to either of the two over a longer period, can calm a patient's anxiety temporarily. The technique has been used in diverse ways for centuries.

Therapeutic effects of electroshock, or electroconvulsive therapy, were first discovered in 1938. The procedure comprises passing electric current through a patient's brain tissue to stimulate an epileptic seizure, after administration of anesthesia. While such treatment was used extensively to treat schizophrenic patients in the 50s and 60s, it fell out of favor and is considered barbaric by many. However, much evidential data support its safety and effectiveness in certain conditions. Patients with bipolar disorder (particularly the manic phase), depression, and schizophrenia appear to benefit from ECT today.

Many psychiatric researchers still aren't quite certain why it works, but according to George Kirov, a clinical professor at Cardiff University in Cardiff, Wales, benefits are hard to pinpoint because the effects are so varied and individual. Jonathon Sadowsky, a medical history professor at Case Western Reserve University in Cleveland and the author of *Electroconvulsive Therapy in America: The Anatomy of a Medical Controversy,* would agree with Kirov. In a 2017 article in the online publication *The Conversation,* Sadowsky claims ECT met an antipsychiatry movement in the 1960s, possibly because of the advent of antipsychotics, and its use declined precipitously. Today, as research evidence becomes available and high-profile celebrity accounts are made public, ECT is gaining a bit of a resurgence. Not without a great deal of controversy, however.

Part of the controversy, acknowledged by critics and supporters alike, is a primary negative effect of ECT: memory loss. There is ongoing debate about how much short-term versus long-term memory is lost, and whether it's regained when treatment stops. These effects are also the most difficult to study and document. It's impossible for me to know what effect the continued use of ECT had on my mother's memory. What I know is that she shared no memories with me. Not one.

A more controversial method used for similar purposes was the sustained, carefully dosed administration of insulin. The goal of insulin shock therapy was to induce a coma. That's why it was also called Insulin Coma Therapy (ICT). It comprised injecting massive doses of insulin, often daily, so that patients entered a coma, sometimes with associated convulsions each day. They cumulatively recorded the length of time spent in a coma each day over a period of weeks. It was typical to achieve fifty or sixty comas, as they considered this the maximum benefit.

ICT was first practiced in 1927 in Vienna, and its use spread rapidly to other countries, including the US in the late 1930s. It declined in use after studies showed its lack of effectiveness and neuroleptic drugs became available, just as ECT therapy was coming under attack as being barbaric. Insulin therapy was later debunked. Experts thought the benefits had been overstated, if they were present at all. Reported side effects included ongoing anxiety and other complications concomitant to the convulsions. Most professionals today believe it should never have been standard practice in treating schizophrenia, but without better options, even brutal treatments became normalized. My father intervened on my mother's behalf in December 1953, presumably because he was aware of the growing skepticism. In my mother's hospital chart, her physician ordered the administration of insulin in varying doses fifty-seven times between August and November of 1953 before discontinuing treatment, at my father's request. They recorded several hundred hours in a coma over a three-month period before it stopped.

Most twenty-first century practitioners focus on future opportunities for pharmacologic treatments for schizophrenia as new drugs become more targeted or more effective in treating symptoms. Because psychiatric patients are notorious for discontinuing their medications when conditions improve, when they lose effectiveness, or when paranoia overrides reason, embedded digital sensors to detect noncompliance may be useful. A few researchers are working on genetic engineering studies because of the genetic component of the disease. However, it may be decades before any such treatments are predictably effective.

Hidden Valley Road, by Robert Kolker, presents extensive, well-researched information about current treatment trends, along with the description of a family in which six of twelve children developed schizophrenia and other psychiatric disorders. The accounts of this Colorado Springs family's trauma, as one after the other of their children succumbed to mental illness, is fascinating as well as heartbreaking. Offering a perspective on evolving research into schizophrenia, Kolker describes several hopeful and ongoing studies.

A promising therapy proposed by Dr. Robert Freedman of the University of Colorado and Editor Emeritus of *The American Journal of Psychiatry* involves preventive treatment in utero. Supplementing a pregnant woman's diet with choline, a substance naturally found in eggs, meat, and some beans and vegetables, which provides properties similar to the neurotransmitter acetylcholine, may assist in the correct development of fetal brain architecture and lead to normal neuron pruning in adolescence. It will take data from several generations before this hypothesis can be proven, but experiments on mice are promising. According to a Freedman 2016 report, the supplementation with choline will only be effective if used during fetal brain development. While it's a potentially straightforward solution to a devastating problem, it would require a massive, sustained educational campaign. It's more likely that a multipronged approach may yet emerge.

Epigeneticists hope that identifying specific DNA methylation mechanisms will lead to antipsychotic drugs that are targeted to counteracting the changes in gene expression that result. In addition, CRISPR technology, a method of altering human genetics, may develop techniques for replacing "schizophrenia" genes. Since the first description of schizophrenia by Dr. Emile Kraepelin in 1887, there has never been a curative treatment proposed, yet biotechnology may provide one. Until then, schizophrenics rely on piecemeal, unappealing, and only partially effective relief of their symptoms.

Having engaged in molecular DNA research during my career, I think current scientific findings hold great promise for both prevention and treatment, but I can't help but wonder if, as a society, we've sacrificed the consciousness of the certifiably insane by soothing the consciences of the presumably sane. Recently, a relative joked at the dinner table about a colleague who visited Central State in the 60s and who was frightened when a resident lunged at his window to either escape or attack. I was stunned into silence by the snickering that followed. I don't think he meant any harm; it was just a joke aimed at an easy target: the lunatics committed to asylums. The sound of laughter at his friend's close call keeps coming back to me. None of those patients deserved their fates, I wanted to say, but the words didn't form until too late. It's clear attitudes have changed little as we've turned toward psychotropic drugs to control the scary behavior most people associate with the mentally ill.

There's a clear demarcation between treatments pre-Thorazine and post-Thorazine, as if there were no value in the physical exercise and productive occupations that patients experienced in the 1950s and 60s because aside from ECT, these were the only options. Maybe restoring quality of life to schizophrenia patients is not a matter of either/or but many/all regarding pharmacology, ECT, genetic, and occupational therapies. I don't doubt that the modern psychiatric institutions of today engage in forms of physical or behavioral therapies, but when I remember the lush, rolling hills, sewing and wood shop facilities, grazing cattle, and productive activity at the Central Louisiana State Hospital my mother inhabited, I'm not sure we've made as much progress as we think. Have we lost a sense of how the patient's environment, including their human environment, affects their mental health? Nature heals, and the instinct to separate from it is itself a disease. Natural environments with predictable rhythms and supportive community can offer a measure of calm serenity and well-being to an otherwise anxious brain.

Residential facilities across the US closed down in droves in the later decades of the twentieth century. They housed close to half a million people in these institutions in the 1950s. Stories emerged of abuses at some of them. Stories of husbands disposing of wives. Stories of mismanagement. These misdeeds were not likely as rampant as some believe; rather, the public becomes restless when tax dollars are spent in ways that don't appear to benefit them. Many of the homeless souls setting up makeshift tents or wandering downtown streets of most major cities—muttering to themselves as they pace at intersections—are likely schizophrenics. Drivers ignore them or shake their fists as they drive by, and city officials hatch plans to "clean up the streets," as a result, calling in law enforcement officers to do the dirty work. I'd like to think human society will someday accept the victims of brain aberrations as deserving of whatever natural and therapeutic means have proven successful, and to make them available to all who could benefit. I'd like to imagine my mother as the fortunate recipient of such possibilities.

Southeast Louisiana Hospital
Henke, Barbara
Hospital Number 201
July 2, 1953

Initial Presentation

This patient was initially presented to the staff on July 2, 1953. Tentative diagnosis was schizophrenic reaction, catatonic type. This thirty-year-old woman has an illness characterized today by marked flatness and inappropriateness and a very diffuse content, mildly paranoid in nature, marked slowing and evidences of confusion and in almost a catatonic stupor while in the interview. She had a previous illness at the time of the birth of her second child. Present illness began approximately ten months ago. Since then, she has had three or four weeks of insulin and, in the recent past, nine ECTs which apparently lifted her confusion so that this was not so apparent at the time of her admission to this hospital as it is at present.

This patient would have both heredity and environmental factors operating from her early childhood in that we have an indication that her sister suffered an early psychotic break and that her parents were always at odds and showed little warmth toward one another or toward the children. If we are to accept the history as being fairly reliable about the patient's function prior to her illness and not too colored by her husband's idealization of what her personality once was, we might assume that this has been a very malignant disease, that she once functioned quite well intellectually. Her confusion is widespread and interferes at times with even the simplest routine. It is felt at this point that a diagnosis of schizophrenic reaction, undifferentiated type best describes her behavior.

Recommendations: The only way this patient can remain outside the institutional environment is if she has someone directly to help her maintain the ordinary household routine.

VI

Ten Months 1958-1959

"Stay there," Karen pulled me back behind her, then peeked out through the tall plumes of pampas grass that lined the east side of our house. It was April 1959, and I was six years old, just finishing the first grade.

"What's happening?" I strained to see around her, toward the driveway, where I could hear screaming.

"Shh!" Karen pushed me behind her again, and I gave in, growing aware of the danger just twenty yards before us. I'd learned to trust my big sister's commands.

Mother was yelling something, but I couldn't make out words. And it seemed she was hitting someone, but my memory is unclear about who. Our brother? Maybe. We heard hysterical screeching, frightening us and attracting the attention of neighbors. I sank down on my heels, clutching the spiny blades of pampas to hold myself steady, the leaves sharp as a well-honed paring knife cutting into my palms. We waited, unseen.

Sometime later, minutes or an hour, Dad drove up in our family's black Ford sedan. Still hiding behind Karen, I saw little of what happened next, but there was shouting, and my father struck our mother—the only time I saw him strike anyone. In my memory, there was a hairbrush involved. Perhaps she'd carried one out of the house. Somehow, the three of us escaped. A neighbor had called Dad at work, Karen told me later. The entire violent and noisy scene was played out in our driveway, as public a humiliation as was possible, and the most permanent lesson I was given about shame. We all learned not to draw Mother's attention, if we could help it. Karen filled in a few of the details in later years, but she was tight-lipped, or perhaps blessedly memory free.

Ever since my mother's discharge from Central State in June 1958, our household had been in turmoil. It was the summer just before I started school, after Karen had finished the fifth grade, and Jon the third. Weekly trips to St. Patrick's Hospital across town for my mother's ECT punctuated our weeks. While she was there, getting her brain reset and her emotions wiped clean, Dad drove us down the street to Borden's Ice Cream for a treat. For some time after each treatment, she was silent and withdrawn, like a parasitic wasp wrapped in a cocoon of its own making, before it emerged, ready to wound again.

According to both Karen and Jon, there were violent arguments at night, with stinging words and accusations. "I remember the loud arguing and screaming in their bedroom many a night," Jon told me, "I think she was scared, and I felt sorry for her but was also afraid that she might come into our room and start screaming. It went on into the night sometimes." These may be incidents I scrubbed from memory. Or maybe I was unaware of them while my siblings feared for our safety.

"Dad was trying to calm her down so she could get to sleep. I really felt sorry for him," Jon said.

Dad hired housekeepers to help our mother manage cleaning and ordinary tasks during the days he was at work, including keeping us kids (and Mother?) in order. Our mother was furious and objected to the housekeepers, though, and none of them stayed long, which explains why I don't remember any from this time. Mother's bizarre behaviors disturbed them, and they chafed at the constant accusations she leveled on them. This may have caused the frequent evening arguments, along with Mother's suspicions about who or what was plotting against her. She thought Dad was trying to poison us all. In the kitchen one morning, she ordered me to stick out my tongue for inspection. Something on my tongue was supposed proof of the threat of poisoning she was convinced we were facing. Karen remembers she made the three of us drink bleach-laced lemonade, and I wonder if it was the antidote Mother presumed would save us.

Just before school began in August, a few months after her hospital discharge, the five of us traveled to Atlantic City to visit Mother's family. Our trip meant we all would miss the first few days of our school year, which involved at least one small attention-drawing spectacle I would become as the "new" kid to class. In New Jersey, we met cousins, aunts, and uncles we'd never known. This was the first time I'd met my Bloom grandparents. They never visited Louisiana, and while we saw our Indiana grandparents once or twice a year, I'd never been to Mother's home in New Jersey. I recall little about the visit, aside from being admonished for trying to give a younger cousin a piggyback ride and being cautioned to be quieter in the house. At just-turned-six, I ignored the older relatives and enjoyed the play with our cousins, most of whom were younger than I was. The visit provided some sense of the family I'd come from—one small puzzle piece, which I relegated to the border, perhaps a corner. Meeting these people created a tenuous relationship with a grandmother who, for a few years at least, sent an occasional letter and a few gifts of clothing that were mostly oversized or unappealing.

I entered first grade when we returned to Lake Charles, the long-awaited education I'd envied the previous years when Karen and Jon left me for their own days of God-only-knew what fun and edification at Oak Park Elementary. I'd spent my days with whoever Dad hired to spend their own days with me, and while most of them were also mothers, I didn't know their children or witness their interactions with them. How was I to know that mothers interact differently with their own children? I was a quiet child, and housekeepers seldom had reason to scold me. They cared about my safety and well-being. They met my physical needs, but there were no expressions of love. *This is the way of mothers.*

I trusted the mothers of our church to want what was best for the children of the congregation, including me. They told us Bible stories and taught classes to foster faith development. They enlisted our help in tasks to teach us responsibility. They gave hugs and friendly greetings. They shared God's love with us. Despite feeling accepted by them, I would never have confided my hopes or growing-girl fears to any of these women, either the ones hired to care for me or the ones who cared for me out of Christian love.

Now that our mother lived with us, I learned that a mother, my *actual* mother, may not always be trusted. Like the women who looked after me, my mother was not a woman to confide in. While she might care for my physical needs as the housekeepers did, she might also exhibit random and bizarre behavior. She might pull a knife out of the drawer and threaten our father, or she might fly into a rage and hurl accusations at the nearest target. Perhaps we shared loving moments during her time in our home, but if so, I don't remember a single one. Did she love me? I cannot say.

My first-grade teacher was Mrs. Hollywood, which seemed an exotic name for an ordinary teacher. She was a kindhearted woman, who seemed old in my limited experience. She corrected us when we were out of line, and I was placed in the corner once for talking too much, along with my new friend Janet. That we found two corners out of view of the rest of the class near the coat closets on either side of the classroom door seemed a stroke of luck. Unfortunately, Mrs. Hollywood discovered it allowed us to continue our previous conversation uninterrupted by the day's lessons. She assigned us a writing assignment instead of our corner-standing penance. A page of "I will not talk in class."

First grade allowed a kind of social interaction I'd never experienced, my first introduction to other kids and other families outside the neighborhood. Mothers were often at school with their children, sometimes in the classroom hosting celebrations or bringing snacks. My education that year included much more than simple math facts and *See Spot Run!* I learned to observe my surroundings and the people in them to plan my responses and temper my demeanor. I learned to pretend I didn't care how different things were at my house.

The confusion took its toll on my digestive system as well. I vomited in class several times in the first few weeks of school—one spectacular event dripped down into the radiator vents—and I suffered frequent bouts of diarrhea. Because I was too shy to ask to go to the bathroom while announcing the required "Number one" or "Number two," this sometimes meant soiled underpants. It seemed I couldn't win; either situation led to embarrassment. I blotted the dark spots with toilet paper in the school's bathroom stalls so they wouldn't be detected. When I got home, I locked myself in the bathroom and rinsed my underwear in the sink to avoid humiliation at home, where it was dangerous to call too much attention to myself. Whether my digestive upsets resulted from lemonade-bleach cocktails or anxiety, I can't say.

I wasn't the only anxious child in our class, and this was at least one small comfort. While I was busy observing and memorizing normal behaviors of my classmates, a few of them were busy dealing with their own worries. Some found paste a delicacy. It smells good and all, but it never appealed to my discerning palate. Then there were the booger eaters. They must have learned somewhere that it wasn't an appealing habit, but they were inventive about concealing their addiction, the way a boozer hides the tiny flask of whiskey inside his boot. I'm sure some kids in the class were well-adjusted, well-behaved, and intelligent, but none of those kids were memorable.

One girl in particular, Marcia, couldn't seem to hold her pencil the right way. Besides eating paste, she insisted on planting her pencil upright between her index and middle finger, instead of resting it on the side of the pointer finger like the rest of us.

In addition, she broke into tears at the slightest correction. No. Actually, the tears frequently came without warning several times a day. It got so bad that Mrs. Hollywood tacked a calendar on the bulletin board and put a star on each day that Marcia didn't burst into tears. In contrast, I coached myself in correction avoidance. I didn't dare draw that kind of attention.

Despite natural shyness and growing fear of appearing abnormal, I made my first friend that year. Janet lived just a block away, and we played together at school or in the neighborhood, but I was curious about what life was like in other homes. Marcia invited me once to play with her after school, or perhaps I just followed her to her home across the street from the school's playground.

It hadn't occurred to me to ask anyone's permission or to make anyone aware of my impulse to follow Marcia home. I'd never had play dates. My siblings and I played with kids on our block in our yards or across the street in the vacant field, but we never felt the need to ask permission. It was the way neighborhood kids played in the 1950s. Somehow, my mother got wind of my unplanned excursion and ended up at Marcia's house to retrieve me. There was a nasty scene, which I didn't witness, in which my mother displayed some kind of irrational behaviors, there were probably obscenities involved, and we scurried home afterward. I was blithely unaware of what my escapade would cost me.

Word gets around, even in elementary school. Marcia never asked me to her home again, which didn't much faze me. My curiosity was satisfied, and who wants to be best friends with a crier who couldn't hold a pencil? However, after that day, aside from Janet, no one else would play with me either. Marcia's mother must have shared the gory details of my mother's tirade. Wary that schizophrenia might be contagious, classmates' parents didn't want me in their homes.

After the dramatic scene in the yard near the end of my first-grade year, word spread to the entire school. That same day, Karen had invited—a little tentatively—her friend Cheryl to come home with her after school.

"I hadn't ever had a friend over," Karen said, "and the first was also the last time." Mother must have somehow felt threatened by Cheryl and shouted accusations at her. Maybe it was Cheryl, instead of my brother, she attacked in our driveway the day she lost her tenuous hold on sanity. I didn't remember Karen's friend at all until she told me this some 60 years later. This outburst would mark Mother's last day in our home and forever represent her character for me. Cheryl left, terrified, while Mother spiraled violently out of control over the next few hours.

Jon remembers a previous day when Dad came home from work. "Mother and he came into the kitchen arguing, she most vehemently, and she opened the drawer, took out a butcher knife, and threatened Dad with it. Dad soothed her and took it away from her, but a few days later, the police came to take her to be committed again.

"The morning they came for her, it was early, and

we were just eating breakfast and getting ready for school when Pastor Hagens came into the kitchen to be with us while Dad and the police got her into the car and took her off. I was terrified." No wonder we tried to forget, even if our schoolmates and their mothers couldn't.

It was one thing for a mother of my first-grade classmate to caution other mothers about allowing their children in my presence, but quite another for a twelve-year-old to relate to every other sixth grader in the school the horrifying events that had befallen her at the hands of Karen's insane mother. While few children would play with me after the outburst Marcia's mother witnessed, none of Karen's classmates would talk to her after Cheryl's dramatic story of her harrowing escape from a lunatic. It took years for the Henke kids to shake free of the gossip, but memory of trauma is persistent—sometimes lifelong.

Did they have good reason to avoid us? I already knew there was something different about my mother, about our family. I didn't yet understand that at one time, my mother had been a girl like I was, a young woman with hopes, dreams, and talents, and later a wife and mother who loved her family and who failed—no matter how hard she might have tried—to prevent her world from breaking apart. That woman was a puzzle I didn't yet care to solve.

In 1959, all I knew was that I might take after a crazy woman, and I'd been exposed to a mother who my father assumed was damaged by her mother and who had the potential to damage us. Despite my father's best efforts, would I end up as she did? Would I catch crazy too?

In the aftermath of those ten tension-packed months and the years that followed, key people would show up to fill gaps when I needed them. I couldn't recognize or appreciate their importance in real time, but they were trailing puzzle pieces all the way.

Southeast Louisiana Hospital
Henke, Barbara
Hospital Number 201
June 25, 1953

Mental Status Examination:

This patient is a tall, brunette woman with attractive features who appears about her stated age of thirty. She shows some carelessness in her habits of dress, and although she pays particular attention to her cosmetics, is inattentive to other personal habits such as combing her hair. Her general mood is one of mild excitement combined with much confusion, but she has been generally able to cooperate with most of the ward routine and enters into the group activities to a limited degree. She remains quite taciturn and somewhat seclusive on the ward.

At interview, the patient is only moderately cooperative, was unable to control her movements, frequently jumping up from her chair or beginning some rather disorganized gesture as taking a match out of the match box to light a cigarette that was already lighted. There was an inconstancy of her facial expressions with the predominance of inappropriate smiling or laughter, but frequently the patient appeared haughty or almost on the verge of tears. She showed considerable restless movement but there were no definite tremors or abnormal motor incoordination observed.

Emotional Reaction:

This patient shows a striking variability in her mood from depression to elation or suspicion and distrust to a rather sticky display of affection toward the interviewer. She was completely unable to describe her subjective feelings and complained that this was worse than before she came to the hospital but could not describe exactly how it was worse. She did reveal that she felt a considerable resentment towards being hospitalized and that the entire situation was strange to her.

Part II

Ten Things I Know About My Mother

1. She was born in Atlantic City, New Jersey, on November 6, 1922, and died at Central Louisiana State Hospital in Pineville, Louisiana, on January 21, 1966.

2. She was the oldest of four children and one of two who developed schizophrenia.

3. She loved to read, ride horses and boats, and play Bridge and Ping-Pong.

4. Blue was her favorite color.

5. She enjoyed writing plays during high school and college.

6. She was an excellent typist and typed my father's papers when he was a student at Purdue University.

7. According to my father, she was fearless when learning new subjects.

8. She graduated in 1944 from Douglass College for Women, New Jersey, in the top twenty percent of her class with a degree in journalism.

9. After college, she worked for George Gallup and the *Atlantic City Press*.

10. She married in August 1946 and had three children (1947, 1949, and 1952).

VII

Barbara

My mother had no control over how her family or the community who cared for us remembered her. Perhaps my father mourned, but if he did, his grief was private. He planned her funeral years after he'd separated us and after trauma soured his memories. I suspect he'd made peace with having lost her long before her death. I'm saddened today by the knowledge that no one sincerely grieved her passing. We all hope to be missed and remembered well by those we leave behind.

I've already picked out a couple of hymns for my memorial service. "Here I Am Lord" gives me chills when I sing it. This hymn, all by itself, once motivated me to make a medical mission trip to South America. "This is My Father's World" because it always makes me cry. I admit it's a little sexist for a woman who believes God is as much mother as father, but we sang it at my grandfather's and father's funerals, and I like that sense of continuity. I've also asked that I be cremated, though I'm still debating what I'd like done with my ashes. Fertilize the garden? I hope to decide before the time comes. I don't want what's left of me sitting in some overpriced urn mingling with dust while my family agonizes over where to scatter my remains.

The larger question is this: How will I be remembered after I'm gone? I'd get the biggest kick out of hanging around long enough to hear the stories people tell about me after I die. You never know what they'll remember. You hope they'll remember how you aced your medical technology certifying exam six weeks after giving birth, but they won't. It's more likely that what sticks in their minds is the time you locked your keys in your car at your daughter's school with a trunk full of groceries, milk and ice cream included, and had to ride the bus home with her. On second thought, haunting my memorial service is a bad idea. No matter what the stories are, the one thing I can count on is stories—some funny, some sad. There will be memories.

Not so for my mother. Documents give evidence of her existence. They consist of birth and death certificates, a few dozen photos, her medical records from one four-year stay in a mental hospital, a college typing textbook, and a handful of other objects. I barely need a second hand to count actual memories of my mother, and a few of those I'd rather forget. Some of them comprise nothing more than brief images or impressions. Otherwise, I have only physical evidence, artifacts. As a result, the "Ten Things I Know About My Mother" is mostly just a collection of facts and impressions given me by others.

The closest things to memories are stories I've been told. A handful from my aunt and my father, a few from my siblings. I know as much about the candidates running for city council this year as I know about who my mother was. When she died in 1966, I was wrestling, at thirteen, with a growing need to understand who she was and who I would be.

Because my aunt was so much younger than my mother, she could offer few memories of their life together, and their other two siblings died long before I garnered the courage to ask. My father was reluctant to tell his stories, maybe reluctant to remember them. My brother admits he's probably consciously forgotten. I'm grateful for each story I hear, but I don't appear in any of them, and there's no one left alive who knew my mother *before*.

Before her brain short-circuited and she became my mother, Barbara Jean Bloom was the eldest daughter of a fairly well-to-do New Jersey real estate developer and his wife. They alternated their time between their home in Atlantic City and a second home in Ft. Myers, Florida. Barbara and her siblings led a privileged life, attending school in Florida during the winters and in New Jersey the rest of the year. Crates of oranges and grapefruit arrived from Florida at Christmastime throughout my childhood, products of the groves I supposed they owned.

It was in Ft. Myers where my parents shared the most carefree days of their courtship, judging from the photos where they're lounging on the beach with sisters and friends. Handwritten dates show the photos were taken in 1944, the year before the Army shipped Dad to Germany and two years before their marriage in 1946.

By all accounts, the only two I have, Mother was an attractive and intelligent young woman; young men sought after her. "Sons of prominent families were trying to date her," my Aunt Connie said, "but her standards were high, and she would not taint her reputation with young men who drank or smoked. It says a lot for your dad that he lived up to the standards of excellence she set and adhered to." It's also ironic, given that one of the few memories of my mother during hospital passes home is of her chain-smoking Pall Malls and chain-drinking Coca Cola, habits I presume had calming effects.

In 1940, when she was near high school graduation, Mother won a scholarship to the New Jersey College for Women, where she earned a degree in journalism in 1944. A *Daily Home News* clipping from her scrapbook shows a picture of a young, serious-looking Bobbie Bloom in a pillbox hat along with her answer to a question posed in the "Inquiring Photographer" column about why she chose the NJCW. Her response seems overly formal to modern ears. "Attending the New Jersey College for Women has been in the back of my mind for a number of years and when I won a New Jersey state scholarship last June it cinched things, so I started to pack and head for New Brunswick," she said. "The cooperative spirit about the campus is very much of an aid to green freshmen and I can foresee a pleasant four years ahead of me."

I sincerely hope her college years proved rewarding. She had no way of knowing they'd be among the last pleasant years of her life.

My parents' marriage in 1946 presented challenges, but wartime must have created havoc for many married couples. "Your Dad went back to finish college after WWII and worked to make ends meet. Barbara, too, worked, and they had to share an apartment during that period with another couple," Aunt Connie told me. Considering my mother's upbringing, it must have been a disappointment. My sister Karen was born in 1947, less than a year after their marriage, and my brother Jon exactly two years later—they share the same birthday.

Photos of my mother with Karen and with Jon show a radiant smile and the proud bearing of a new mother showing off her brilliant progeny with friends and family whom I can't identify. After Jon's birth in 1949, hints of difficulty appeared, possibly indicating postpartum depression, and placed her at higher risk for future psychotic episodes. By 1952, the year of my birth, a diagnosis of schizophrenia loomed. I have one photo of my mother and me during my infancy, and she's not smiling. There are a handful of photos that include the two of us after that date, during passes from the hospital at

Christmas or ordinary weekends at our home, and neither of us is smiling in any of them.

I have only a few images of my mother in Lake Charles. She received weekend passes to our home from the hospital occasionally. According to her hospital records, there were over thirty passes authorized between 1953 and 1957, but I don't know how many she took. Dad transferred her to Central State in 1957, and I have no records aside from two index cards of data from the hospital—and very few memories—from the last eight years of her life.

Of her sporadic visits home during the late 50s, I remember only snippets: lying on the bathroom floor and peering under the door to see what she was doing inside. Sitting spellbound on the oak wood floor while she cut fabric from paper patterns with dressmaking shears for garments that were never sewn. My mother turning from the front seat to slap my brother's face in the back seat of the car without saying a word. Making me open my mouth so she could inspect my tongue for evidence of the poisoning she was convinced someone was perpetrating on us. The last scene etched in my memory is the day she came unglued in the front yard during my first-grade year, after a ten-month stint in our home, and after which she remained hospitalized until her death. None of these incidents or any of the visits we paid her on holidays or weekends include words in my memory, though they must have been uttered.

After what I've learned about Mother through the evidences—the random puzzle pieces—I've been given, there are nagging questions: Would I have liked and respected this woman? Who would I have become if I'd grown up with her? At the descriptions provided by my Aunt Connie of Mother as status conscious, relatively wealthy, and having belonged to the "right high school sorority," I cringe. These descriptors are anathema to my life, as my father taught us that wealth and status are more likely to corrupt than lead to satisfaction. Had my mother been able to parent me, would I have learned different lessons or become someone else? Would I be someone for whom mention in the society section of the newspaper was important? I'll never know how our relationship might have shaped me. Instead, her absence molded me in ways I can't quantify or analyze. The shapes of gaps she left in the puzzle can be instructive, too.

Among the memorabilia I guard of Mother's life is the only surviving example of her heartfelt words, in a brief letter written to my father three days before her death. When someone asks, "How did your mother comfort you when you were sick?" or "What was your mother's greatest wish?" I don't know how to respond because I honestly don't know the answers. If pressed, I will choose the words she used to end her letter to my father in January 1966, which didn't arrive until she was already gone: "Love you dearly. Waiting to hear from you." These are the words I hold closest to my heart.

Another piece of evidence I protect is the guest book from Mother's funeral, when I was thirteen. My paternal grandparents, who had moved to Lake Charles not long before this, were the only relatives in attendance. Our Bloom grandparents—Mother's parents—sent flowers. There are roughly eighty signatures of fellow church members or work colleagues, Janet's parents, Karen's college boyfriend and future husband, and a few neighborhood friends. There's no record of the funeral service other than the guest book and a copy of her obituary. I don't recall the hymns my father chose for the service. The stories told were stories of the Henke family, but not about Barbara Jean; few in attendance had ever met her. Our family was well loved by these people who bore witness to my mother's life and death. However, they couldn't provide insight into the mother I might've had. If I were to solve the puzzle of Barbara Jean Bloom, I'd have to look elsewhere for the pieces.

Southeast Louisiana Hospital
Henke, Barbara
Hospital Number 201
June 25, 1953

Content of Thought:

Due to the patient's quite disorganized verbalizations it was difficult to determine any logical progression of trends in her thought content, although she made numerous illusions to ideas of persecution by her husband and her father. She explained that she was brought to the hospital because she wanted to go visit in Atlantic City but denied that she could explain why this had happened to her. In addition, she admitted that she had wanted a divorce but could not decide whether this was the reason she was brought to the hospital or whether her husband brought her to the hospital in order that he might obtain a divorce. She was likewise confused about whether her husband or her father had been responsible for her commitment. She also stated that she has lost several objects since she has been in the hospital but refused to explain whether she felt these had been taken from her by other patients or by hospital personnel.

She mentioned suggestive hypochondrial ideas by inquiring several times whether her chest X-ray and Wassermann were negative or not and stating that she was quite relieved to find they were negative. She alludes that her illness is presently due to the lack of men and believes her sexual inactivity is causing her to be more disturbed.

She expressed ideas of unreality and that everything seems strange to her and repeatedly requested to know exactly which way was north, east, south and west, or to know what direction the hospital is from Lake Charles, and which direction she traveled in coming here. She revealed no hallucinatory experiences, refused to answer any questions with regard to these, and showed no definite depressive or grandiose repair. When questioned about her plans directly she replied that she felt she needed guidance but could not elaborate upon this.

VIII
Gold Dust Twins

"Your hair is so golden, it glitters in the sun like gold dust," our third-grade teacher Mrs. Sibley explained after dubbing my friend Janet and me the Gold Dust Twins. She suggested we use that pen name for the stories we wrote together. We were delighted by her attention and giggled over the stories we composed on the wide-ruled notebook paper we stapled together; I don't remember a single plotline. Janet was the illustrator since I couldn't draw recognizable stick figures. Our authorial skills flourished under Mrs. Sibley's approving eye. I'd been comfortable with earlier teachers, but none had captured my devotion in the same way. Mrs. Hollywood was nice enough, but life at home was too chaotic that year, and my embarrassing digestive upsets were so unnerving that I couldn't settle in. Miss Martin, in second grade, was young, pretty (she had a *boyfriend*!), and well-liked, but I suspect she was inexperienced and didn't challenge me. Mrs. Sibley was the first teacher I fell in love with for her kindness and the encouragement she provided.

By this time, my mother was ensconced in Pineville, where she remained until her death, and where we visited every few months. This arrangement made it easy to pretend I didn't have a mother, and I sometimes fantasized about having a mother like Mrs. Sibley. In this fantasy world, she would've walked me to school and home each day, sometimes holding my hand. She'd have helped me with lessons and been proud of my precocious reading ability. We'd have baked brownies together, she in a white cotton apron with a ruffled skirt and me licking chocolaty, delicious goo off my fingers. There would've been silly knock-knock jokes and sidesplitting giggles, singing at bath time, and invented stories featuring me as the heroine. I would've had a personal cheerleader to inspire confidence while I mastered the times tables or memorized the weekly spelling words.

Nowhere in this fantasy world did I imagine a scolding or a harsh word, even when I failed to carry my dirty plate and fork to the sink after dinner or when I ruined my shiny, patent leather Sunday shoes by defying her order to not wear them outside to play. Never would Mrs. Sibley have made me sop up the water I splashed onto the bathroom floor while pretending to ride in a submarine. On no occasion would she have forced me to eat liver ... or peas. If my daydreams about Mrs. Sibley spilled over into the classroom, and if I sneaked a few secret smiles in her direction, she gave no hint she suspected her part in my imaginary life. Instead, she guided me through third grade with generous good humor, and I loved her for it.

Eager to curry Mrs. Sibley's favor, I was an annoyingly clingy suck-up. My grades were good, but the needs improvement checks on my report card show I needed to develop better self-control and the ability to work independently. What didn't show up on my report card was my diligent practice at appearing normal so that none of my classmates would have reason to gossip. Blending in was my top priority and my greatest talent. I laughed at the same jokes as everyone else, even the taunting insults: "Somebody better call Pineville. One of their lunatics is missing!" I learned well how to mimic the words of other kids.

In 1961, when I was in the fourth grade, I joined the Bluebirds, the junior version of Camp Fire Girls. A classmate's mother and our group's leader, Mrs. Kevil, showed us how to complete our merit badge tasks, and I accumulated several that I sewed, somewhat crookedly, onto my sash by myself. Before long, it became apparent that some moms who provided rides felt imposed upon. Unable to articulate my discomfort at not fitting in, I quit the group. I crammed the sash into the back of my dresser drawer and pretended it didn't matter that my mother never picked up friends for a meeting, chaperoned our outings, or demonstrated a skill the way Mrs. Kevil had.

The fourth-grade year created more academic challenges as well. "Oh no! Not Mrs. Sims!" we'd cried when my peers and I got our new class assignment. Mrs. Sims wasn't popular with students because she was strict and businesslike. Anxious about moving from a classroom where I was secure, and where I knew my teacher cared about me, I groaned along with the rest, but I set about learning what I'd need to get by without attracting undue attention. I obediently memorized my multiplication facts and read everything my developing skills allowed.

Mrs. Sims was an older woman with a gray bun of hair and a no-nonsense manner, but she was fair. That year, I learned it was possible to both respect *and* like a teacher. If students were serious about learning, Mrs. Sims was serious about giving them tools to succeed, and I'd always been serious about learning. As my abilities improved, my reading material became more substantial. We had books at home, but I'd never seen as many as Mrs. Sims kept on her classroom bookshelves. She encouraged us to take books from the shelves each week and gave us class time to read, which was ecstasy for me.

The book I remember best was a small encyclopedic paperback book about snakes, with color pictures and descriptions of their habits. It might seem a strange choice for a ten-year-old girl, and I don't know what attracted me to it, but it cured me of a fear of snakes. When something slithers out from under my tomato plants while I'm weeding, I'll jump like I've been bitten, but it's out of surprise rather than fear. Two things I remember from my study of snakes: they're more afraid of me than I of them, and they eat a lot of the insects I despise. Like cockroaches. I'm *terrified* of the giant flying cockroaches that haunted the first twenty-four years of my life. That's one fear this south Louisiana girl hasn't ever grown out of. Learning about what I'm afraid of may be an effective way to face my fears, but I don't see myself picking up a book on cockroaches. My love of learning from books has its limits.

In fifth grade, we spent most recess periods playing softball on the playground, a large, grassy field adjoining the school, with a short, oval track and bare patches of dirt to form our bases. Every so often, teams realigned, and team captains chose players. Captains were always boys—the girls ceded athletic prowess early. Once, during team realignment, Jimmy chose me for his team, and I was thrilled. He was my first almost crush, and being chosen (*second*, no less, and before many of the boys) was a heady experience. While I was a decent runner, my batting resembled swatting flies. I could hit the ball, but not well, and I more often tipped it or hit fly balls. I probably struck out every time at bat on Jimmy's team, but it didn't matter. I'd been chosen.

I was wary of my fifth-grade teacher, Mrs. Reed, who was more glamorous than my former teachers, and to whom I never really warmed up. Yet I recognized something about her I aspired to: a sense of self-confidence and a way of moving about the school and the world as though she belonged. If I loved Mrs. Sibley and respected Mrs. Sims, I admired Mrs. Reed. She was attractive, trim, and animated. She had a pretty, popular daughter a little older than we were. The daughter, a cheerleader at the junior high, sometimes joined her mother in our classroom after school. I was not like either of these females, but observing their close relationship fueled my sense of what I'd missed.

A year later, in 1963, the Friday before our Thanksgiving break in sixth grade, the school secretary broke into our classroom after lunch. Her face was drained of color. "The President's been shot!" she announced, and she hesitated in the doorway for a moment, eyes wide and mouth standing open, as though she wasn't sure what to say or do next. After a silent pause, she gave her head a shake and said, "I just don't believe it," before moving on to the next classroom.

Our teacher, Mrs. Dyer, lived nearby and rushed home to get a television set so we could watch coverage of the unfolding events. The class was subdued. We'd all seen people shot on television Westerns, but we were old enough to understand the dramatic difference. At first, the only sounds came from the television. But soon, up and down the rows, students murmured or moaned in reaction to the account of events on the screen, graphic descriptions of what the Dallas crowd had witnessed. Stunned shock gave way to fear.

We heard reports of the presidential motorcade in the moments before and after that morning's gunshots, events which reporters and historians would rehash and debate all afternoon and into the next century. They rushed the President to Parkland Hospital in Dallas, just down the street from the research hospital I'd work in as a medical technologist forty years later. Our class watched the television coverage with nervous tittering and fingernail chewing for word of the President's status. The entire country held its breath. Soon, we learned Kennedy had died. Mrs. Dyer cried into a tissue and said little, her attention held captive by the account of events on TV and the disbelief that had gripped the entire school.

Girls sobbed, and even the boys scrubbed at damp eyes, which perplexed me. I held my back straight, stared straight ahead at the television, and pleated my skirt over and over between sweaty fingers before smoothing the fabric over my knees. Sandra and Becky didn't know this man, Mr. President Kennedy, did they? Why were they crying? I hadn't ever known anyone who'd died and wondered how I should feel, what my classmates felt. With a tight chest and knotted stomach, I contemplated a man smiling and waving one moment, slumped and unmoving the next, as the newscasters described him. It was unsettling, but I'd learned not to cry in public, not to display emotions. It attracted too much attention.

Mothers came to school in droves that afternoon. Cars clogged the street in front of school, driven by moms who lived just down the block and typically walked their children home. The parents were dazed, but they made sympathetic noises and hugged their sniffling children to comfort them. I hung back longer than usual, sensing the same fear and confusion in the adults that had overwhelmed my classmates. Amidst the chaos of parents and children finding each other and clamoring toward the safety of their homes, I felt invisible.

I trudged home, mulling over the events of the day and everyone's reactions to it. My eyes might well have been the only dry ones in the classroom. At home, Dad was in bed, asleep.

"I got sick at work this morning," he said, "and I came home early to rest." Jon and Karen weren't yet home from their junior high and high school, so he hadn't heard the news.

"President Kennedy got assassinated!" As soon as the words left my mouth, I burst into inconsolable weeping. Dad gave me a tissue and put his arm around me while I blubbered. "We heard it on TV. He's dead!"

Dad broke his own rule that forbade watching television before dinner and flipped on the old black-and-white set. News coverage drew us to the screen like iron filings to a magnetic field.

That evening, when I calmed down, and after

our somber dinner and television news updates, Dad said, “the President wasn’t exiled. He was assassinated.”

“That’s what I said.”

“You told me he was exiled. Exiled means they made him leave the country.”

“I know what it means,” I snapped, “He was assassinated.” That Dad thought I didn’t know the difference offended me. By the time school resumed after Thanksgiving break, our collective shock had ebbed, but my world no longer seemed safe.

Southeast Louisiana Hospital
Henke, Barbara
Hospital Number 201
June 25, 1953

Sensorium, Mental Grasp and Capacity:

This patient is oriented to place and person but could not give the date or estimate the time. She likewise complained of recent memory defect but could give the hours of her departure from home, and arrival here, although she did not know how long this had been or on what date she arrived. She was completely unable to cooperate with most of the formal testing, replied with tangential associations to questions put to her or refused to reply to any other questioning. From the history it would appear that her intellectual function has been above average prior to the onset of her present illness, and the patient's vocabulary would suggest a rather high degree of education, but it is difficult to determine what her present intellectual function is.

Summary of Mental Examination:

This thirty-year-old housewife presents symptoms of marked confusion, disorientation and disorganization of her mental activity at present. She shows a mild degree of excitement with a variability of her affective responses and apparent inconstancy of her moods not appropriate to occurrences in the external environment. The confusion and disorganization predominate her content of thought at present but shows a suggestion of widespread delusional ideas of persecution and somatic delusions centered primarily about her sexual organs. Her sensorium is cloudy and she was unable to cooperate with the formal testing, so that an evaluation of her intellectual function is not possible at present, but her abstraction shows a definite impairment.

IX
Private Spaces

Mrs. Sibley might have thought my hair looked dusted with gold, but my bowl cut was never stylish. No one in our house was gifted in hair arranging. There were no ribbons, bows, or braids. Only bobby pins and the pigtails my small fingers could scrunch into place with rubber bands from my school supply box. Though we were always clean, with hair and teeth brushed, hair arranging and fashionable clothes were of little importance. My siblings and I selected our wardrobes from the JCPenney or Sears catalogs, as there was no mother or aunt or grandmother to take us shopping in the local stores. Instead, we ordered our annual school clothes well before the first day of classes in August. We tried them on for fit at home, where they were folded and tucked into drawers or hung in our bedroom closets.

The house on Eighteenth Street in Lake Charles had a walk-in closet, which was a novelty in the 1950s. During the thirteen years our family lived there, it served alternately as a den or a bedroom. It was my bedroom for a few years in the early 60s, but it had been a playroom or den through much of the decade prior. During her brief stay with us in 1958 and '59, my mother clipped fabric in the shape of paper clothing patterns on that floor. I sat near her, mesmerized by her movements. I can still hear the characteristic swish-swash of sewing shears against the oak planks and see my mother's hands working each stroke, one of only a handful of specific memories of us together. Perhaps she stored the patterns and the fabric in the closet, along with other family treasures. There might have been a sewing machine, too, but no finished garments ever materialized.

A single, high wooden shelf spanned three walls of the closet. The shelf was deepest along one side, just above the hanger rod on which hung out of season clothing, Karen's and my school dresses, and one floor-length plastic garment bag. Against the wall, opposite the door, was a chest of drawers. The shelf held my mother's hatbox, our board games, and boxes of photos. On the floor, in the far corner, my father stashed his film developing and printing equipment.

When I was young, the closet became our hide-and-seek headquarters. We sometimes played games on the bare wood floor among the family mementos. I invited friends to help organize schoolrooms for our dolls or in later years, to plan romances with Barbie and Ken. I also loved reading in the silence of this space. There were books lined up on the narrow shelf across from the clothing bar, and some of my earliest memories are of devising ways to reach them. Karen found me once on the closet floor with one of them, doing my best to unlock their secret code of letters.

"Silly!" She turned the book right side up with a giggle, "You can't read it that way."

Dad's copy of *A Child's Garden of Verses* and another with scary stories he often read to me at bedtime about ghosts and hobgoblins were among the books I remember. I also remember *Grimm's Fairy Tales* and was captivated by Hans Christian Andersen's tale of "The Red Shoes," because I had a much-loved pair of red shoes myself. A hardback novel called *Never Look Back* sported a paper jacket with a skull and dagger on it that kept me awake at night as I lay in my bed with the door closed tightly between us.

In the far corner of the closet, tucked back on the top shelf out of view—where it took standing on a chair to retrieve them—was a file box of photographs. Photography had been my father's passion since high school, when he was an officer of the Photography Club. Later, while he was a student at Purdue University, Dad worked part-time as a surgical photographer to earn tuition money.

Dad photographed surgeries, wounds, and

tumors, along with variously afflicted body parts. More than one depicted sexual organs, at least one we presumed to be a sexual act. How could my siblings and I know which ones were normal and which were not? Despite knowing we were forbidden access, we studied them with both fascination and alarm. *Oh my God. Not that. Not there.*

My brother, sister, and I were drawn to them like rubberneckers to a train wreck.

When my mother came to live with us in June 1958, the closet became a quiet refuge from the chaos she sometimes orchestrated elsewhere. I'd compared mothers of classmates and friends to the one who had just moved into my father's bedroom. Mine didn't behave like theirs did; she hadn't met with my teachers and didn't brush or braid my hair. She didn't shop with me for Sunday dresses or shoes—not even the shiny patent leather Mary Janes I longed for—and didn't offer to drive my siblings and me to the Roller Rink. In fact, my mother didn't drive our family's black Ford sedan. These were things other mothers did. It was confusing. In the private, dark closet space, I contemplated the reasons for my mother's odd habits and why she'd just now come to live with us. Perhaps it was my fault she was sick. I knew she'd left when I was a baby; maybe I'd been a bad-tempered baby. I found it comforting to sit, unseen, beneath the hanging clothes, wedged between the plastic garment bag and boxes of familiar keepsakes.

My mother's clothes filled the zippered garment bag. There were woolen sweaters and shoes and an ankle-length fur coat. The fur was soft and dark brown, almost black. It's the same coat my mother's wearing in a couple of photographs I have of her during her courtship with my father in New Jersey and their early married years in Indiana and Ohio. One thing I know for certain: she never wore that coat in Louisiana. It hung unworn in our closet during the thirteen years she lived in Louisiana mental hospitals, and Dad discarded it along with her other clothing after her death. I knew my mother only from visits to the hospital on Sunday afternoons, Christmas day and other holidays, from a few turbulent months in our home. Her fur coat was a relic from *before*. Who was the woman who'd worn this coat? Where had she gone?

After Mother's schizophrenia came raging back, only months after it had abated enough for discharge, the police escorted her back to the hospital to stay. Several years later, I moved into the room she'd once cut patterns in. I'd reached adolescence and stopped inviting friends into my closet to play school or to plan romances with Barbie and Ken. I was too old for Barbies, and I was old enough to value keeping what separated my life from the lives of my friends a secret.

In those private moments, I sometimes still unzipped the garment bag and slipped my hand in to touch my mother's fur coat, to bury my fingers in its softness, and to rest my palm against the shell, testing for lingering warmth. I sometimes leaned in to inhale the familiar scent of her and wonder what had gone wrong. Years after being enclosed this way, separated from the rest of us and our everyday lives, her clothing didn't smell of cologne or sweat or the cigarette smoke that encircled her much of the time she was with us. It smelled like my mother's skin, and it dredged up a longing I couldn't identify.

Southeast Louisiana State Hospital
Barbara Henke
Patient # 201
November 20, 1953

Insulin Therapy Notes

This patient started treatment on August 28, 1953. She finished on November 20. She had a total of sixty insulin treatments with fifty-one comas. She had no secondaries while on insulin treatment. For the most part her treatment was uneventful. She first went in to coma at 260 units, finished at 310 units. Her highest dose was 420. She showed some clinical improvement through therapy and was increasingly flat in disposition. However, her basic pathology did not change. The patient apparently had a secondary the night of October 12, or the morning of October 13. No other was reported. She, on occasion, went very deep but would lighten rapidly. She went very deep on September 16 and had a very hyper-excitable period on November 6. The patient received 2,195 minutes of insulin coma or 36.58 hours.

Ten Things I Know About My Father

1. Because he said my mother once told him he didn't look good in blue, he refused to wear blue clothing for the next 50 years. We buried him in a gray suit in 1994.

2. Each night when I was a child, after reading to me and tucking me into bed, he said, "Goodnight. Sleep tight. Don't let the bedbugs bite."

3. He took us kids to visit his parents in Indianapolis once or twice a year, spending one night at the same Holiday Inn in Memphis, Tennessee, in each direction.

4. He took a woodworking class once and built a coffee table and a set of bunk beds, which furnished our home for years.

5. During the second semester of my freshman year in college, Dad drove me to an 8:00 chemistry class and cooked an omelet for us both every one of those days.

6. He valued literature and education. A few years before his death, he packed up a set of around fifty Little Leather Library classics from his childhood and gifted them to me.

7. He smoked cigarettes for decades, switching to cigars (safer), and a pipe (even safer), before quitting altogether. I can still smell the Dutch Masters tobacco he tamped into his pipe.

8. He built a greenhouse shelf garden at the home he shared with my stepmother. It overflowed with pencil and Christmas cactus, aloe vera, and more,

and from which he shared cuttings.

9. He and my stepmother often traveled to the Southwest US, and he left an extensive collection of treasured sand paintings and Native American pottery after his death.

10. He often sent newspaper and magazine clippings to his nine grandchildren, along with a brief letter telling them why he thought they'd be interested.

X
Fred

It's a peculiar characteristic of children that they cannot see their parents as individuals, only the mother or father they became. I assumed I knew my father as closely as anyone did and more so than many. Certainly, I could share more than ten things I know about him, ten things that portray the kind of person he was, unlike what I know about my mother. However, despite my deep and abiding love for him, I admit there's much I don't know about Fred Henke.

While sorting a box of family photographs recently, I discovered a photo among dozens of others taken during Dad's tour of duty in Germany during World War II. I'd seen this one before and tossed it in the pile with the others, categorizing them as Dad's "war years." It wasn't until 2020 that I read the stamped date, May 30, 1945, and Dad's handwritten inscription on the back: "Broadmoor Hotel, Col."

The iconic Broadmoor resort opened in 1918 to great fanfare with a golf club and luxury amenities at the base of Colorado Springs' Cheyenne Mountain and poised at the edge of Cheyenne Lake. It has hosted presidents and celebrities and has been the site of dozens of professional ice skating and golf tournaments, as well as a 2003 NATO summit. I don't know if my father brushed shoulders with any of the dignitaries or witnessed any of the events hosted there in 1945.

In the faded and spotted color photo, Dad's wearing his Army uniform and familiar wire-rimmed glasses, sitting on a wooden rail, and grinning at the photographer. Behind him is Cheyenne Lake and the unfocused edifice of the Broadmoor. There are several military facilities in the area, so perhaps he attended a training session before he shipped out to Germany.

Since 2009, my husband and I had traveled to Colorado Springs three times to be with family—my brother Jon and his wife Trudy owned a vacation condo there and often shared it with friends and family. We'd been aware of the Broadmoor's existence but had paid little attention. I didn't know of this fragile connection to Dad until I looked more closely at the photo. During a 2020 visit, we attempted to survey the resort and lake from the same vantage point my father had assumed. At the heart of the Broadmoor grounds and the edge of Cheyenne lake, where Dad had been photographed in 1945, I posed for several snapshots 75 years later. A glance at our Broadmoor portraits, now side-by-side above my writing desk, fills my heart.

"I got shot in the butt, and they sent me home," was all Dad would say about his Army combat service. He'd enlisted in 1942 and was discharged in January 1946 at the rank of Private First Class. It's not clear how long he served overseas; it may have been a few short months before that stray piece of shrapnel pierced his flesh.

A scar was the only obvious effect of his injury. I suspect the pain of that hole in his butt paled when compared to the sorrow he encountered not long after returning to civilian life: completing university, marrying, starting a family, institutionalizing his schizophrenic wife against her will a few years later, then caring for their three young children on his own through more than a decade after.

The 1945 photo is a reminder of a younger, happier man who dreamed of a different future. His smile is radiant, broad with the promise of life with the woman waiting to marry him once his service ended, as broad a smile as I'd seen in the 41 years he was my father.

I wish I'd known the man in the picture.

After Army basic training in 1942, they transferred Dad to New Brunswick, New Jersey. He enrolled in classes at Rutgers University, and in the fall of 1943, he attended a mixer with other soldiers and students from sister school Douglass College for Women. It was there he met Barbara Jean Bloom. She was vivacious and outgoing enough to draw Dad out of his usual quiet self and into a world of parties, summers in Florida, and relative wealth. For the next two years, they spent much of their time together before the Army intervened.

Dad left for Germany in 1945 and didn't return until being wounded and released from active duty several months later. My parents married in August 1946 and moved to West Lafayette, Indiana, where Dad finished a chemistry degree program at Purdue University, around the time my sister Karen arrived in 1947. Most of what happened between her birth and mine, five years later, I had to learn on my own. Dad didn't tell family stories; he preferred reading us fairy tales or fantastical adventures from storybooks. Maybe they seemed safer.

In 2005, when I received copies of some of Mother's hospital records, I encountered my father's story for the first time. His words painted a painful account of his and my mother's marriage after the births of their children. According to the history provided by my father at her first hospital commitment, Mother seemed pleased with motherhood after Karen's birth, but less so after Jon's. Her moods changed often, becoming hostile occasionally, and she sometimes lost track of large chunks of time. Perhaps she suffered from postpartum depression.

For a time, her symptoms resolved or decreased. She'd taken an interest in meeting neighbors and seemed to form several friendships in Cincinnati after moving there in 1948. The trouble started around 1950, when Jon was a toddler. Bouts of paranoia plagued her, but there was no tangible cause and no obvious remedy. Still in Cincinnati, my mother became pregnant for a third time. Soon her symptoms could not be ignored, as her behavior became more irrational; they also became diagnosable.

I read how my mother had seen me as damaged from the beginning, with the dark blotch of a birthmark on my forehead and my inverted feet, an anxiety that evidently consumed her. In September of that year, a month after my birth, Dad took a position at W. R. Grace Chemical Company in southwest Louisiana. As if there weren't enough to worry him, Dad had to find and purchase a home, seek psychiatric treatment for his wife, and tend to three children, one of whom—me—was only weeks old. Dad's parents stepped in to help, and my mother, siblings, and I spent a few months in Indianapolis at their home. Mother checked into a private psychiatric hospital for treatment, but despite improving slightly after insulin shock therapy, her overall condition regressed. We moved as planned near the end of 1952, and not long after, Mother was committed to the hospital four hours away.

The situation might have broken a lesser man, but our father was not such a man. He took on the roles of father and mother, immersing himself in caring for his children, church work, and a few hobbies like photography and fishing. Maybe he hoped that a recovered wife would someday rejoin us, a hope that surely withered and died over the next several years.

During my childhood, Dad maintained darkroom equipment in our garage or utility room, where he developed and printed his own photos. Dozens from his tour of duty in Germany survive, as do several photos of my mother with my siblings. In one picture of my mother alone, she's lying on her side with her head propped in her hand and staring at the camera with a pensive look, whatever she might have spoken before or after lost to time. There are only a handful of myself as a child, likely a consequence of more complicated times. The gaps in timeframe between prints don't allow a full accounting of the family I was born to, but these photos tell their own story. Reading his words in Mother's chart, over ten years after Dad's death, gave me a clearer picture of all he'd suffered before and during her early hospitalization. They provided a glimmer of who my mother had once been and chronicled her descent into madness, which we each survived in our own way.

My father's style of parenting fell somewhere between that of his own depression-era upbringing and recommendations from Dr. Spock, the parenting expert du jour in the 50s. He was easygoing in his care, but there were non-negotiables. Mealtimes were consistent, as were bedtimes. We never questioned attendance at church services, choir rehearsals, youth group activities, or regular church building and grounds maintenance. Schoolwork was a priority. Aside from these few parameters, Dad often left us to roam the block or hop a city bus at the corner to go downtown. There was no coddling, no hugging, no verbal expressions of love. The exception was the simple goodnight kiss on the cheek after a bedtime story until I was nine or ten and decided I was too old for such childishness.

"You don't need to come," I told Dad one evening at bedtime, "I'm going to bed now."

"Okay," he said, puzzled. After a small hesitation, he added, "Goodnight."

I was proud of my first step toward autonomy. What I don't know is which of us was more disappointed in my minor victory. I tucked myself in to my single bed—alone—and cried myself to sleep.

While Dad didn't actively play with us as a mother might have, he *provided* for our play. He built a stile for me to cross the fence behind our house, so I could visit my friend Mara on the other side when I was in grade school. When the stand of bamboo outside our back door grew out of bounds and beyond his expectations, he thinned out the center to create a play world in the middle of our backyard. My siblings and I engaged in imaginative games in what we considered our "playhouse." Jon and his friends sometimes acted as soldiers while Karen and I nursed their invented injuries. It's near impossible to kill bamboo once it takes hold, but

Dad cut it back occasionally, so we could make use of the hollowed-out grove for years until we tired of playhouses.

Dad did his best to provide motherly care as well, but he was uncomfortable with raising daughters. He hadn't learned to cook or keep house when he was growing up; there was no need in a traditional young man's life in the 1940s. As a result, he was determined that his son would learn more about such things, although he had few of the skills needed to teach any of us. He was woefully inept as a cook. Instead, he and Jon enjoyed fishing and camping together, as fathers and sons have done for centuries. Dad was active in Jon's Boy Scout activities, too, shepherding him all the way through his Eagle Scout project. Afterwards, Dad was a leader of Jon's Explorer Scout troop. "I felt kind of bad for you and Karen," Jon once told me, "I felt like I was monopolizing Dad's attention, but I loved it."

Perhaps Dad was content to let the women he hired or the women at church model feminine habits with his two daughters. He brought Karen and me fishing now and then, but he was clearly unprepared for some aspects of our maturation process.

"You don't need a bra," Dad said behind the closed door of his bedroom when I was in sixth grade, "You will, soon enough, but not yet."

I was mortified. Everyone knows that, at age twelve, any discussion of brassieres should be confined to the schoolyard among girlfriends and definitely not with your father. I couldn't speak.

"Where'd you get it?"

"Janet and I bought it at Perry's," I said, studying my shoes. We'd pooled our money and gone in halfsies during a recent visit to the five and dime in the neighborhood and intended to take turns at wearing our purchase.

"Well, give it to Janet. You might need a girdle before you need a bra," he said with a pat on my butt.

Red-faced, I mumbled assent and fled. I couldn't imagine how he knew what I wore under my shirt. The bra was a modestly sized, firmly padded 32AA. In hindsight, I admit it probably stuck out like two coconut halves against my otherwise flat chest. By the time my breast development required a bra, I was well into junior high school and a perfect size 32AA, the late blooming I'd counted on never materializing.

After the violent months of angry and threatening arguments we witnessed in 1958 and '59, when our mother lived with us, my siblings and I rarely pushed our limits. Like Jon, we all felt sorry for the anger Mother aimed at Dad, and we didn't want to add to his grief by being unruly. While Dad didn't yell, utter harsh words, or exact punishments, there was no mistaking his disappointment when we failed to live up to expectation. He could quietly, and with few words, make me disappointed in myself. At the same time, he infused in the three of us a sense of responsibility and compassion for others.

Dad admitted to shyness, a trait he passed on to

me. I also inherited from him a deep sense of curiosity about scientific investigation, which he encouraged. The chemistry set he gave me for Christmas the year I was ten remains the best Christmas gift I've ever gotten. It was a complete surprise and infused with a sense that Dad had given me a part of himself. He'd brought me to his lab at W. R. Grace a few times, let me sit at the desk in his office, and pretend I was in charge. I wrote official-sounding memos and arranged his pens and pencils into neat rows, being naturally uncomfortable with disorder. I sat up as tall as my years would allow in Dad's chair while his employees humored me by calling me "Miss Henke." The chemistry set was even better, because this gift was meant for me, *not* my brother or sister. This man whom I adored, but who hadn't ever said "I love you" shared his Chief-Chemist self with me.

The chemistry set wasn't sophisticated; it was designed for children. But I made crystals, and I mixed various elements or chemicals together to create new compounds, according to the lab directions in the printed pamphlet that came with the set. Some compounds smelled of rotten eggs or the sharp, choking odors I associated with the chemical plants near our home in southwest Louisiana. Phew! One or two billowed out dark smoke! Some experiments simply didn't work. While the pink volcano was dramatic, the crystals were miniscule, and CO2 bubbles didn't appear when expected. Yet this minor act of confidence in my aptitude set the stage for my professional life.

"I don't know how to do this," I said. It was a March morning in 1994, and I was explaining to a colleague at the American Red Cross what I'd started and what she'd have to finish after I left.

When a coworker called me to the break room phone a few minutes before, my brother Jon greeted me with, "Good morning, Jan," and I was delighted to hear his voice. We didn't see each other often and rarely talked by phone since we lived in different states, over an eight-hour drive apart. I remember thinking it odd that he'd called the particular phone number he had since there was a phone on my desk. It didn't occur to me I'd never given him a work number at all. I never expected him to need one.

"Hi Jon! How are you?"

"Jan, Dad died this morning."

My legs were too weak to hold me, and I slid into the nearest chair while he gave me the sketchy details he'd been told by Karen a few minutes before. About the sudden heart attack. About how Mom had gone to the hairdresser, and it took a couple hours to get word to her, and ultimately to Jon. About when the family would arrive in Lake Charles. "Call Mom," he said, "and see if there's any more she can tell you."

I called my husband as soon as I got back to my desk, but my voice was shaky, and it took a couple of tries to put the word "dead" in the same sentence with "Dad." He could tell something was wrong at the outset, but he assumed I was calling to give him unwelcome news about his own father, who wasn't in good health and nearing ninety. My Dad had just turned seventy. "I'll head home in a few minutes," he told me, and I was left, every body cell trembling, to explain my unfinished work to others.

"I just don't know how to do this," I said again.

As a quality assurance team in a blood bank, we certified blood as safe for transfusion, and I took my position seriously. Those critical tasks suddenly seemed trivial. I was reluctant to leave, though. Gathering in Lake Charles with the rest of the family to mourn my father's death would force me to confront a pain I wasn't ready for. I didn't know how to do this new thing, accept as final the death of someone who held such importance in my life, or how I'd live the rest of my life without him.

When I got home, I called my parents' home number, expecting to tell Mom that we'd arrange flights as soon as we could. Our son Marc would have to drive over from Dallas, but Tim and our daughter Kelly and I would be there later in the evening. Instead of reaching Mom, who was attending to the obligations of survivors, I got the recording on their landline's answering machine. It was Dad's voice, requesting that I "leave a message after the beep tone." That's when I broke down.

My family had grown considerably by 1994, and we all converged at the family home to meet with the pastor about the memorial service. Dad had remarried less than a year after Mother died in

1966 to a widow named Ruby, who my siblings and I immediately called Mom. Like me, everyone who gathered that evening was in shock.

"He'd just had a stress test in December," Mom said, "The report was encouraging." After suffering a minor heart attack at age 62, Dad retired so they could enjoy some travel. In fact, they were preparing to leave town for a bus tour when Dad went to the church to install a scrolling lighted sign in the fellowship hall for the congregation's fortieth anniversary celebration taking place in their absence. Dad collapsed in the middle of his task. Another member of the church—a nurse—was there also, and she saw him fall.

"She started CPR immediately," Karen said, "By the time the ambulance arrived a few minutes later, though, he was gone."

We submitted hymns and scripture verses to the pastor that we wanted for the service. I don't know why this title popped into my head. I don't think it had been a favorite, but I requested the traditional hymn "This is My Father's World." We hugged each other and cried. "This family is full of love," the pastor said with a smile before she prayed with us. My family had been steadfast members of the church for most of its forty years. "We'll miss Fred."

My sense of shock extended through the next few days, the visiting hours at the funeral home, and the service itself, which was also our daughter's eighteenth birthday. At the end of the service, the pastor called me aside. "You know, I thought your choice of hymn was a little odd for a funeral service, because it's a hymn of praise," she said, "but it was just perfect to end the service that way. Your dad would have agreed."

I stayed in Lake Charles a couple of days after Tim and our kids left. The last night at Mom's house, we were looking at photo albums of her life with my father laid out on the dining room table, and we remarked over the years of memories recorded in those photos. It was surprising to me that there were so many. Almost thirty years' worth, which by then represented most of my life. Those were years Tim and I lived in Texas or Oklahoma, while our children were growing from youngsters to adolescents and into their own personalities. While we were going about our own business of being a family and while Dad and Mom had lived their marriage and grown to be best friends, time I was glad they'd had together.

This was the second time Mom had been widowed, both husbands dying suddenly, without her knowing the last goodbye was final. We talked of goodbyes, of children growing up and moving away.

"Kelly will go off to Texas Tech in a few months," I confided, "Marc has a job in Dallas now and supports himself." It was what we'd prepared for, this launch of our children into the world. "I always thought my job as a mom would end when they left home. They're both adults now, and I thought I could stop worrying about my kids when they were adults."

Mom smiled and put her hand over mine. "Your Dad worried about the three of you until the day he died."

A few days later, when I was trying to get back to

normal in Oklahoma, to a life that seemed anything but normal, I filed a copy of Dad's memorial service bulletin along with the others I'd saved from funerals over the years. When I pulled out the bulletin for my Grandfather Henke's funeral ten years before, also conducted in St. Paul Lutheran's sanctuary, I realized which hymn my father had chosen for *his* father's memorial service: "This is My Father's World." Indeed.

Whatever distress I'd felt at the time of my father's remarriage had mellowed over the years, but it now took on a despondent, permanent quality. My father was an integral figure in my life for over forty-one years, and I couldn't fathom the world without him. We'd only recently learned to say, "Love you," at the end of phone calls between our home in Tulsa and his home in Lake Charles. While I'd never doubted his love for me, hearing the words uplifted my spirit. It took me months to accept that I wouldn't hear them in his voice again.

Southeast Louisiana State Hospital
Barbara Henke
Patient # 201
June 10, 1953

Anamnesis [an account of a medical history]

The information for this anamnesis was obtained from the patient's husband, Frederick R. Henke, a tall, prematurely balding, and bespectacled man who appears to be about his stated age of twenty-nine. Mr. Henke was quite attentive and cooperative at interview, appeared to show a genuine interest in the patient's welfare, but showed very little insight into her condition and tended to be circumstantial in the information he gave. He explained that he had always been very shy himself, and that even in retrospect, he could not be certain what his wife's reactions had been to certain events.

Personal History

[The patient] is described by her husband as having been very ambitious, she used to talk about wanting to write for newspapers, she has done some writing for the radio, and at the university, she wrote several plays. He states that she seemed a sociable person, was usually a little more forward than he had been, and took an active part in community affairs. She liked to go dancing and drink beer but was used to more entertainment than her husband could provide when they were going together since her parents had more money than he had had.

The patient's husband believes that the strict moral code the patient's mother enforced upon her caused the patient to have anxieties even for her husband to kiss her when they were first dating.

The patient and her husband went to live in Lafayette, Indiana, while he was completing his work at Purdue, and for a short time she worked in one of the offices of the university. She became pregnant during the second month of their marriage, and the husband states that although they had not planned to have a child so soon, the patient seemed to be pleased at having a child, although she was a little moody at first during her pregnancy. Their first child was born in July of 1947, a girl named Karen. The second child, a boy, Jon, was born in July of 1949, and although the husband states that he did not notice it at the time, some of their friends have remarked that the patient seemed slightly depressed after this baby was born.

Within a year, however, she became noticeably withdrawn, complained that she did not believe her neighbors were fit to associate with, and became very class conscious. Although she retained a few friends, she took less interest in community projects, seemed to worry more about the children and was more irritable at home.

The patient's husband dates her present

illness to about one month before her last baby was born in August of 1952. At that time, she became markedly depressed, complained that she felt tired out, and cried a good deal. She was worried about the baby's condition before it arrived, and afterwards it was noted that the baby had a slight inclination to turn its feet in, as well as a birthmark on its face, so the patient was distressed when her obstetrician recommended that the baby should be examined by a pediatrician. Her obstetrician gave her a mood-lifting drug which seemed to help for a while, but when the effects were lessened, she was even more upset ... By this time the patient was so confused, depressed, and disorganized that she was completely unable to do anything about packing or moving.

Since January of 1953 the patient has been depressed, is irritable, and accuses her husband of infidelity. By March of 1953 she was not able to sleep, could not eat very much, talked about wanting to leave her husband and go off and leave her children, and felt that people were insulting her even when they were complimenting her... Dr. Funk started the patient on out-patient electroconvulsive treatments, and she received six in three weeks' period in March, and showed some improvement ... After about two weeks following discontinuation of the treatment however, the patient's condition returned to about the state before the treatments were started, and it was necessary to give her nine more treatments in April. When the effects of the second course of treatment appeared to be wearing off, it was recommended to the husband that the patient be committed, and she was brought to this hospital on May 25, 1953.

XI
Little Fish

You know those nightmares about fumbling to open a jammed locker on Monday morning, in nothing but your Friday underwear, and late for the history test you forgot to study for? Yeah. That's what the first weeks of junior high felt like in 1964.

My friend Janet and I and the rest of our classmates moved on to Oak Park Junior High, a few blocks north of the elementary school. If I thought starting first grade was fraught with anxiety, seventh grade was worse. I was now thrown into a much larger pond with new, bigger fish species. Introverted and shy as I was, meeting new people had never been my strength. There were compensations, though. Merging with seventh graders from other schools and school days spent with several teachers a day instead of just one provided relief. I could keep my history and my home life private. No one else at junior high admitted they had parents anyway.

Despite my efforts to project an aura of confidence, junior high introduced embarrassments and failures. I was nominated for Miss Courtesy, but I wasn't elected. Still enamored with my fifth-grade teacher's cheerleader daughter, I took her advice to make a name for myself. I lost in a landslide against a popular older student. School had become my proving ground, and I persisted in efforts to distinguish myself. I made good grades, consistently made Principal's Honor Roll, and snagged perfect attendance awards each year. I had a group of friends with whom I could be myself, without fear of being discovered as the daughter of the "loony tune" that my peers warned against in earlier grades. The vagaries of the female body confounded me, though. I'd never had it betray me as it did one day when I was thirteen.

There I was, among hundreds of other eighth graders, caught off guard with enough blood in my drawers to begin a tiny red stain on the back of my pale yellow dress. For a timid young girl, an unexpected period at junior high school is a crisis. Intensifying my panic was the memory of one classmate's recent humiliation: she bled so fiercely through her clothes in biology class that when she got up, Mrs. Lane suggested she swab the seat with paper towels before the next class could sit down. I don't know how she managed it; I would've had to transfer to another school.

The school nurse was sympathetic but not all that helpful. After she'd given me a sanitary pad—sans belt—she suggested I call my mother to bring me a change of clothes. It was the sort of suggestion that *seemed* reasonable enough, but it was impossible. I could not make myself explain to a woman I didn't know that my mother was a resident of the state mental hospital in Pineville. Divulging such personal information in earlier grades had taught me to keep my mouth shut. At a minimum, it made people nervous, as though my genes were diseased and infectious. Instead, I responded, "My mother's not at home." I would've bled to death before I'd have called my father. As far as I knew, he wasn't aware I *had* periods.

I had a better idea. "Can I call my friend's mother to come get me?" The Davenports lived in the house catty-corner behind ours, and their youngest daughter was a classmate. I knew Mrs. Davenport would be home; she didn't drive their only car. When I called, she agreed to come get me, which meant walking the five blocks to our junior high school to sign me out and then to walk me home.

I'd often thought Mrs. Davenport should've joined a religious order, instead of marrying a cantankerous man and having four loud and quarrelsome children. She and her children were devout Catholics, and I went with them to Mass a few times. Mr. Davenport worked shift work at one of the nearby chemical plants and was often sleeping or at work when I was at their home. I was terrified of him. I'd once witnessed his yelling and throwing an entire pot of green beans out the back door onto the grass because his wife had unthinkingly added bacon to them one Friday, a day that good Catholics fasted from eating meat. Even at thirteen, I knew this didn't qualify him as a man of faith, but it just might qualify his wife as a saint.

Mrs. Davenport looked like the religious women who lived in my imagination. She had a fair complexion, reddish blonde hair, and a sprinkling of Irish freckles across her nose. Her hair was always demurely braided and coiled on top of her head, where she pinned her lacy head covering for Mass on Sundays. She was calm and soft-spoken, as quiet as her family was loud.

I don't recall our conversation the afternoon she walked me home, but I remember feeling surprised to discover that someone cared enough to walk all the way to school to get me. She walked me to my driveway and waited while I went inside before continuing around the block to her own home. I'm not sure I thanked her, though I like to think I did. What I didn't tell her was how significant her small mission was; I didn't know it myself. As a motherless teen, I delighted in opportunities to spend time with mothers I admired, but I didn't know how to articulate that admiration.

Halfway through eighth grade, in January 1966, my mother died of cardiac arrest at Central Louisiana State Hospital. She'd just turned 43. Her death certificate also lists epilepsy as a contributing factor. Because ECT could cause violent seizures, many of which resulted in injury reports on my mother's hospital chart, a fatal seizure is a possibility. She sought medical attention several times for cuts and bruises from falling out of bed after various treatments, or from hitting her head on floors, walls, or bed rails. Some incidents required stitches; most caused bruises. It's also plausible that one of those seizures resulted in cardiac arrest. However, I know she didn't suffer from epilepsy. My take is that she died of treatment for schizophrenia, but that didn't fit well on a death certificate. Perhaps the medical staff was trying to protect her, and us—maybe even themselves—by recording a more acceptable, purely medical condition as contributing to her death.

The greatest irony is that Mother's death brought only a sigh of relief from us. Dad had suffered through a chaotic twenty-year marriage to a seriously ill wife and never expressed anger or disappointment during her hospitalization or after her death, at least not in my presence. He said almost nothing about our mother at all. For my siblings and me, this meant that instead of having a crazy mother, we had *no* mother. I preferred the latter. I was almost proud to disclose this as a reason no one had ever seen my mother, and from that time forward, the only explanation needed was that she was dead. No other details were requested or offered. Some expressed sympathy for my loss, as though loss was something new to me.

"What do I put here?" I asked one teacher when

filling out a high school course selection form that asked for my mother's name and occupation. "My mother's dead."

"Just put her name and write 'deceased' after it." For once, I was happy to be among peers who had suffered similar circumstances.

A few months later, Dad announced he was marrying Ruby Lundgren, a widow with three daughters. Their November marriage was a surprising, but welcome development. I'd just started ninth grade. Ruby's youngest daughter and I were friends, and her mother had ferried us around from swimming pool to skating rink to bowling alley ever since they'd joined our church and shortly after the death of Ruby's first husband. Finally, we would have a mother. And she was *normal*! Yvonne and I attended Confirmation classes together at church. My friend would be my sister! How lucky could I get?

I hadn't expected Dad would ask me to transfer to another school, closer to our new home. Yvonne was also in ninth grade and attended LaGrange Junior High, one of the feeder schools for LaGrange Senior, which our older siblings already attended. Yvonne would stay put after the move, but it was much farther from Oak Park Junior High, so I agreed to transfer to LaGrange. I knew it would make transporting us easier, but I never thought to ask why I was the only one expected to change schools.

"You'll love my teachers. I've told everyone you'll be coming," Yvonne said. It seemed her friends were eager to have me join them, and it was flattering to feel wanted. I knew we'd be moving on to the senior high in a few months. My old classmates and friends would attend a different high school across town, and we would be forced to part ways at that point anyway.

My new Mom drove me to school to accomplish the transfer. I first withdrew from Oak Park, but when I tried to enroll at LaGrange Junior High, they refused. We didn't live in their district. If students moved while enrolled, they could remain enrolled throughout the year, but new students must live in the district, which I no longer did. I couldn't re-enroll at Oak Park. That meant Yvonne could continue at LaGrange, but I'd have to enroll closer to home at Forrest K. White Junior High, where I knew no one. I was unprepared to be the new kid in ninth grade for the last half of the year. While I'd prepared myself for a transfer, this one was so far off the radar as to be across the globe.

"I didn't know," Mom said when we got to the car, surprised by this change in plans. "We'll go home," she offered, although school was still in session. She sneaked glances at me, as though she feared I would break into sobs or blame her for the outcome.

"It's okay," I set my jaw and stared straight ahead, eyes focused on the road all the way home, blinking to clear my vision. *I will not cry*.

I went straight to the room Yvonne and I shared, closed the door, and lay face down on my bed. I thought about my sister moving through her classes at LaGrange, expecting me to drop into her English or biology class before the day was over, thoughts that brought fresh tears.

"What happened?" Yvonne threw her books on her bed and came to sit on mine. She was almost as disappointed as I was. She'd been expecting me to show up in her classes all day.

"I can't go to LaGrange." My tears had dried, and I tried to pretend it didn't matter. "I'm going to F. K. White." It never occurred to me, or anyone else, to suggest that Yvonne transfer with me to further ease the transportation burden. I suppose it was reasonable to displace only one of us but added to the changes I'd already encountered within a matter of weeks, this additional displacement devastated me.

I learned to ride a school bus filled with total strangers, something that horrified me. My best defense was to pretend I didn't need any new friends, and my strategy proved it's at least sometimes true that you shape your own destiny. It felt as though I'd been abandoned in a foreign land where I didn't speak the language. I flirted some with the boys because that seemed easier than letting myself be vulnerable enough to be rejected by any of the girls. I tried to survive until May. At that point, I was so traumatized, I couldn't make the next transition, either. None of my Oak Park classmates were at LaGrange, and none of the students at F.K. White had become friends.

I'd welcomed the promotion to junior high, with its shining promise of more freedoms and new relationships, within the familiarity of my old life. But the unplanned school transfer separating me from my friends—coinciding with the transition to a new home and family—spun me out of a comfortable, dependable orbit into uncharted territory. It wasn't unlike the forced separation my mother faced after my birth. That my father was less available and ensconced in new relationships while I struggled to recognize their contours left me feeling disoriented and misplaced, as Mother must have felt when brought to Central State.

Those nightmares about the locker and the underwear and the test? It seemed the anxiety might finally manifest, and I'd lost my center of gravity.

Southeast Louisiana Hospital
Henke, Barbara
Hospital Number 201

Selected Psychiatric Notes
Special Psychiatric Notes and Orders

May 25, 1953:

This 31-year-old woman has three small children at home ... She has been sick for more than a year and is chiefly confused and seems to be so preoccupied most of the time she can't be certain where she's going or what she's doing. Help her as much as possible to orient herself about her routine and encourage her interest in activities. She is receiving Insulin Coma Therapy.

January 23, 1954:

Patient has unpredictable outbursts of open aggression to patients and personnel, making it inadvisable to have her on C-3 for the time being.

August 23, 1955:

Patient up, asked for cig at 4:30 am. Patient sitting in day room smoking 2nd cig. Patient stated, "I just can't sleep." Patient seemed to be sleeping before 4:00 am.

4:45 am: Patient still sitting in day room smoking 3rd cig.

5:30 am: Patient laying on her bed, awake.

XII
Ruby

She was their mother, not mine. My three new sisters were her *real* daughters, not me. This idea ordered my relationship with my stepmother from the day it began in 1966, even if the fact was pertinent only to me. I was aware of a definite shift in the power structure when my father remarried, and I dared not make assumptions, but I picked up on what I considered subtle clues. It was in the straightforward way she talked to her own three daughters, in carefully chosen words for me. In time and through close observation, I sensed proper responses to gain approval; I was terrified of rejection. Not a biological daughter, I resolved to be a *good* one, an obedient one. My hopes for a mother had been realized, and I would *earn* my place alongside my new sisters. Ruby became *Mom*—the name I chose to call her—and she was going to be the mother I'd never had.

Ruby Lundgren had been widowed just a few years when she and Dad married. Dad often commented that my stepsister Yvonne and I had gotten him and Ruby together for the Henke-Lundgren merger of 1966, or "the merger," as we referred to it. My oldest stepsister Chris married just before the merger, and my sister Karen married a couple of months after; we moved across town to a new, larger home. The arrangement couldn't have been more perfect for the girl who'd spent her formative years wishing for a real mother, could it?

Reality often conflicts with hope, however. In actual families, one sister's penchant for staying up late with all the lights on in the bedroom disturbs the other's need to sleep in a darkened room. A mother's expectation that her daughters, never the son, help maintain a spotless house, vacuuming under beds, along with starching and ironing pillowcases and table linens, seemed unreasonable. It was no longer possible to have a friend sleep over as there was no room, particularly when one sister loathed the other sister's friend. Confusing household rules governed food choices, appropriate dress, behavior, and daily schedules.

At fourteen, I was used to a degree of autonomy. Karen commuted to classes at the local state college, and Jon was busy with high school friends and their rock and roll band, basketball, and scouting activities. What I did after school or what I snacked on weren't closely regulated. After the merger, I began homework when I got home and ate limited snacks that appeared miniscule when compared to my appetite: an apple, for instance, or a small bag of the potato chips that were bought in bulk packs for Dad's lunches. Coca-Cola was poured from two-liter bottles after dinner—one glass each. Quantities and choices never seemed enough, and any limits rendered the options unsatisfying. "You'll ruin your supper," was the reasoning, but I'd never had trouble eating my supper after my previous free-range snacks. Given the wholesome meals Mom cooked versus what we'd cooked for ourselves, I was certain I could eat a healthy meal a few hours after a PBJ. But that wasn't an option. Now that I run a household, I appreciate the attempts to control grocery costs for a family whose size had doubled, but my bruised young heart gave rise to a hunger the approved snacks couldn't satisfy.

There were rules of dress and behavior I'd missed, that other girls must've learned when growing up. It was gauche to wear white shoes before Easter or after Labor Day. I must wear shoes or slippers at all times, indoors and out. Going barefoot outdoors could mean contracting "worms." I tried to imagine them burrowing their way through the bottoms of my feet, an idea that fascinated me. I must hang some shirts on hangers, while I could fold others in drawers. I should fold towels in half, then into half again, then into thirds before placing on linen closet shelves. Folding in half twice, as I'd done previously, was not appropriate. Men's button up cotton shirts must be wrinkle free before wearing, and my sisters and I starched and ironed Dad's and Jon's Oxford shirts and linens on Saturdays. We couldn't leave the house until we completed chores and ironing.

Once I began dating, it was not appropriate to sit too close to a boy on the sofa when the living room drapes were open, because the neighbors might "get the wrong idea." I learned how to introduce people properly, how to answer adults courteously, and when it was polite to keep quiet. "Ladies don't burp," Mom admonished me once, after I'd done just that, demonstrating I was no lady.

I was encouraged to address adults as Ma'am or Sir. These courtesies denoted respect for elders, yet when the people who pronounced these rules uttered racial slurs and called Black adults by their first names, I was confused about who was worthy of respect. Sometimes the instructions were stated, sometimes not. One indirect message infused all other lessons, intentional or not: my life before had been inappropriate; *our family* had been inappropriate. The occasional rebuke, the occasional disapproving looks, reinforced this.

When Yvonne asked to borrow one of my favorite shirts a second time—the yellow "poor-boy" t-shirt that was in style—I told her no. She must have appealed to her mother.

"She didn't wash it like she promised after the last time she wore it," I explained when Mom asked me about it. While my response seemed logical, it was clear my refusal was unacceptable; I felt judged as obstinate and selfish. These and other unspoken censures hurt, but we could both be hurtful.

A couple of years later, I wrote a letter to both parents complaining about what I considered their lack of trust and their refusal to let me date a young man several years my senior. The text of the letter is mostly forgotten now but the intent is not; I intended my words to hurt, and I was too cowardly to speak them. I left the letter on their bed. Dad calmly and quietly—as was his manner—asked me to apologize to Mom the next day. It pains me still that I didn't, but I didn't know how.

Though her expressions of displeasure stung, Mom's kindnesses could also sometimes bring unexpected joy to my heart. She was careful to treat each of the three girls under her roof equally. My sister Yvonne bemoaned that tendency while I appreciated it. "Why do we always have to get the same thing?" she cried after opening her set of luggage at high school graduation. I can't remember what color her set was; mine was green. My transistor radio was blue, my dishes were gold, and my set of pots and pans was red. Mom's commitment to equity in gift giving made me feel like one of her girls.

Eager to become the cultured woman Mom expected of her daughters, I embraced lessons in etiquette and social acceptability, along with instruction in the domestic arts of cooking and sewing. Mom was a patient teacher, who relied more on demonstrating technique and ad hoc cooking than strict adherence to recipe directions.

"Here's how much shortening you need to start your roux." She'd plop a big dollop of Crisco into a hot black iron skillet, and we'd watch it liquefy. "You want about the same amount of flour, too." And I'd watch her sprinkle flour from a scoop into the skillet where it sizzled in the hot, melted shortening.

"Don't let it burn." She'd let me stir the mixture while she watched.

She'd add more flour or Crisco, in random, unmeasured amounts. "It needs a little more thickening," she'd say or, "it's too thick." I kept stirring, while the flour browned, worried it would get too dark. I'd let it burn once, and it took hours for the stench to fade with all the windows open and the vent fan on.

"How will I know it's ready?"

"When it's the color of dog poo." Whenever I demonstrate roux making and repeat this graphic comparison about gauging the darkness of roux, I can still hear Mom laugh at her own description.

Ruby had been born into a Cajun family, for whom preparing roux was a sacred act. "Cajun" is a slang term for an ethnic group, the Acadians of French descent who immigrated to Louisiana after their expulsion from Nova Scotia in the 19th century. There's an old Cajun joke about assessing whether a Cajun girl from a good Catholic family was qualified to marry an upstanding Cajun boy. No matter how extensive the girl's qualifications were, the most important question the young man's mother could ask was, "That's fine, but can she make a roux?" I'm proud I can now make a decent roux.

Holiday baking was also a well-renowned annual tradition. This was one ritual I latched on to like melted sugar on a shortbread Santa. I didn't remember a single homemade cookie at our Eighteenth Street home. In contrast, Mom dared not be embarrassed by a shortage of fresh treats when a drop-in visitor arrived during the holidays. She engaged all of her girls to fill every cookie tin and plastic bin with sweetness that seemed to last from one occasion to the next. This is where I learned to appreciate food as a love language. I'll never mix up or roll out Mom's pecan butterball cookies without thinking of the woman who taught me to make them.

I don't know if any of my mother's sewing attempts included garments for me, but if so, nothing productive came of them. Mom sewed clothing for me before I took over most of my wardrobe construction in high school. The pants and jacket she sewed for me one Christmas was plaid wool, a deep brown and gold houndstooth check with a hint of maroon—I wore it throughout college. Such tangible evidence of Mom devoting time and attention to giving me something that pleased me was another introduction to motherly care that I didn't appreciate until much later. While I'd taken home economics class in ninth grade and had sewn an uncomplicated cotton jumper for myself that year, I didn't learn to sew well until Mom showed me how.

She taught sewing in much the same way she taught cooking: through patient and careful demonstration. On one occasion, I was sewing a jacket from the once-popular, double-knit fabric and pressed the back of it with an iron that was too hot. The synthetic material—essentially glorified plastic—scorched, causing both a fabric and iron operator meltdown.

Mom looked at the heat-puckered cloth and, after a quick inspection, she said, "We can fix it." She showed me how to cut out the ruined half of the back and stitch in a new piece of fabric with a seam down the middle. "Nobody will know that seam isn't supposed to be there." The incident was a valuable lesson in troubleshooting.

However much I valued Mom's instruction in becoming a well-behaved and proper young lady of some accomplishment, there was resentment of her position and lingering pain over what felt like abandonment by my father. It seemed as soon as the ink dried on the marriage certificate, he relinquished control over most household matters and enjoyed new traditions, like the half hour martini and mellow conversation with his new wife before dinner. I wanted him to be happy, but I felt I'd lost something in the bargain and grieved the closeness we'd once shared. Perhaps a hidden part of me felt Mom had stolen him from me. I was never denied access, but Dad's time was now focused on forming new relationships, and I feared it meant giving up the old ones. The sudden diffusion of his attention stung. When Karen married only months after Dad and Mom, and Jon graduated and left for college less than a year later, I felt all the more alone.

My new sisters had lost their father a few years before and might have felt similarly bereft. We mourned in our own ways, I suppose. As was my typical habit of keeping emotions to myself, I stuffed the feelings of resentment, shame, and rejection down inside and tried, with limited aptitude and perhaps a bit too much drama, to play the part I'd chosen for myself as the good, obedient youngest daughter.

Besides being perplexed by this blended, unfamiliar household, I'd gained a huge extended stepfamily. Mom had kin throughout the southern part of the state, who appeared from time to time for boisterous gatherings. There were crawfish boils and seafood gumbos, to which stepaunts, stepuncles, and stepcousins gathered to delight in Mom's hospitality. They often included a rollicking card game of Bourrée. Mom's mother, whom we called "Mamere" (French for Grandma), was a tiny, but spunky woman who spoke Cajun French with her children and heavily accented English with the rest of us. Mamere was an expert Bourrée player and taught all of her grandchildren, including me, how to play. I'll best remember her at the card table and can still hear her laugh, with her slender hand daintily covering her mouth, when she or any of her pupils played a clever hand. She was a kind soul and a beacon of calm in an otherwise bewildering sea of new relations.

After having had no extended family within hundreds of miles, I wasn't sure what to do with the noisy gatherings and occasional tensions. Ordinary exchanges could sometimes be awkward, with perceived metamessages, and I worried how best to respond. This was where my education in family dynamics began, and I was an uneasy student. These people were not my people. My mother's family was across the continent, all the way in New Jersey. My mother might have been psychotic, but I reserved the right to claim the Bloom clan as my own and to invent characteristics for them that best suited my needs.

Visits had been infrequent with my Henke grandparents, too, until the highway department uprooted them from their Indianapolis acreage, and they moved to Louisiana when I was thirteen. The merger took place only months later, before I'd learned to make room for even this one set of grandparents. Conforming to an unwieldy family of dozens, instead of the family of four I'd grown up with, was exhausting, and I dreamed of escape as vividly as I'd once dreamed of having a mother. Now I had a mother, and I was learning how to connect with her while simultaneously struggling to assert a separate, personal identity. My efforts to claim independence could be hurtful, and they were sometimes met with hurtful responses. In addition, I suspect I was using a godlike-mother yardstick to measure her performance. Perhaps Mom was wrestling with her role as mother to three teenage girls; maybe I wasn't the only one challenged by the merger of 1966.

Tim and I married in 1971, and our son was born the same year. A few years later, after our daughter's birth, we moved one state away, then two, returning to Louisiana only once or twice a year. After a while, the distance in miles led to healing of former wounds, as Tim and I built lives that reflected our priorities and needs. During visits, I could maintain my character part for a few days at a time and sincerely enjoy the company of my complex, merged family. After my father's sudden death in 1994, we visited less. It was painful being in the home on Ashland Street without my father. Our children grew up, and we were all busy with careers or school. I was grateful for the love and companionship Mom had shared with my father and I loved her for all she'd meant to his motherless children; we shared a common history, if not always common interests.

In 2008, when Marc and our daughter-in-law Ruth announced they would name their daughter Ruby, several mixed emotions resurfaced, and not only because of the delicate relationship with my stepmother. Ruby Josephine simply seemed a long and complicated name for such a small human.

For a while, we referred to "Big Ruby" and "Little Ruby," and I found the distinction humorous, as did Mom. In a strange way, Ruby Jo made it easier to relate to my stepmother, who often asked about Little Ruby's exploits, perhaps remembering a youth as Little Ruby herself. Mom's health deteriorated and her memory for current details faltered; my attitude toward her grew tender. We'd hurt each other over the decades, and avoiding judgment seemed reason enough to keep my distance. However, it took me almost that long to understand that while I'd felt judged as inadequate, I had also judged Mom for her inadequacies. As the mother of two and grandmother of three, I was finally learning who a mother could be, and I discovered the job was rife with hazardous pitfalls.

In late summer of 2018, I was preparing for another busy fall of classes at the community college where I'd been an adjunct professor for twelve years. I was also anticipating a ten-day vacation to Boston and Maine a couple of weeks before the semester's start. It was the first real vacation Tim and I would have alone in over a decade and would cap off my summer before another school year began.

Just before the semester's start and the week before our vacation, I booked a flight to Lake Charles to see the family. My sisters Karen and Chris and two sisters-in-law still lived there. I felt a sudden need to see Mom, who was then living with Chris and her husband. She'd been hospitalized a few times earlier in the year with infections and dehydration and was now in hospice care. I booked last minute flights for an extended weekend visit.

Mom was quite frail, but her hospitable attitude never changed.

"Do you want anything to drink?" she asked, between shallow breaths. She readjusted the oxygen tube resting below her nose. "Or to eat?"

"No, Mom," I said, kissing her cheek, "I'm fine, but thanks." She repeated the greeting each time I arrived over the next few days.

On Sunday, while the rest of the family was at brunch, I stopped in to visit Mom and her sitter. Mom's nails were still fire-engine red, and her hair was neatly combed, even though she hadn't made it to the hairdresser in months. Her weekly hairdresser appointments had been sacred time all the years I'd known her.

"This is Kathleen," Mom said, motioning to the woman who'd let me in the house. We exchanged pleasantries.

"This is my baby daughter, Jan," Mom said to Kathleen, and her introduction startled me. She'd never referred to me this way, and the tears in her eyes when she said it struck me later as either nostalgic or regretful, maybe both. Kathleen and I discovered a few common interests for light-hearted talk, and while Mom's voice was weak, she smiled to let us know she was enjoying the surrounding conversation.

On Monday morning, I had a midmorning return flight and stopped by one last time. Mom had taken a bad turn overnight. The hospice nurse was there, and she called the chaplain. Some of her grandchildren left work to come by. It appeared her hours were numbered, and I faced a decision to cancel my flight and return my rental car or go home as planned. Tim and I had flights scheduled to Boston on Friday, but I was conflicted.

My sisters all urged me to go ahead, "Mom would

want you to go."

My husband encouraged me to stay, "We can postpone our trip. You'll regret it if you don't stay."

"Mom's always done right by me," I said through tears when Chris put her arms around me, "I want to do right by her."

I canceled my flight and turned in the car. When my nieces and nephews came, and we gathered with the chaplain for prayer a couple of hours later, she rallied. She talked a little and smiled at our weak jokes. Before she left, the hospice nurse warned us privately that she'd noticed signs of a "death rattle." My sisters and I planned on taking turns for an overnight vigil. I would take the nine to midnight slot so Sue and Chris could rest. It proved impossible for them to sleep, but I was alone for a time with Mom. Breaths came with such long pauses between them, I glanced over to assure myself another would follow. A bit later, both sisters joined us again, and we told stories about times we'd shared in earlier days and sang familiar hymns or listened to gospel music videos on my phone.

My sister Sue, who'd lost her husband the previous year after a lengthy illness, cautioned that Mom could linger in this state for hours or days, and I decided around midnight to get some sleep. When I slid into bed at my sister-in-law's house across town a few minutes later, I was exhausted but wide awake. The call came early the next morning: Mom died on July 31, a few weeks before her 95th birthday and only minutes after I'd left for the night.

Tim was right that I'd regret not staying through

to the end. Spending time with Mom in the last few days of her life and speaking at her memorial service were honors. I've often thought of my place in the family Mom and Dad built from a merger that included six teenagers and realized a grief I hadn't felt at my mother's passing. A complex set of factors kept me from acknowledging—for 52 years—the mother I'd always wanted. I'd resented "losing" my father to a loving partner and was likely jealous of Ruby's relationship with the daughters she gave birth to. We were imperfect people, and we'd both been critical of each other's shortcomings. Despite the challenges we'd negotiated, even the roadblocks I set up, Ruby Henke had indeed done right by me. I'm not sure I ever earned the title of *good* daughter that I sought, but I feel privileged to have been Ruby's *baby* daughter.

Southeast Louisiana Hospital
Henke, Barbara
Hospital Number 201
July 11, 1954

Return from Convalescent Note:

This patient was placed on Convalescent Status on April 25, 1954, and was referred for follow-up to the Lake Charles Mental Hygiene Clinic because of the long distance to travel for return appointments. She was seen there on three or four occasions by Dr. Kraft who reported to us that she did not seem capable of remaining at home. Her husband phoned the hospital during the week preceding her return, on July 11, 1954, explaining that it was impossible to care for her at home and arrangements for a bed were made.

At the time Barbara returned she was reluctant to reenter the hospital but was cooperative. She was oriented and seemed in better contact than at the time of her initial admission but complained of the housekeeper at home and felt she was being "bossed" too much. She wept in talking about this and showed some fragmented persecutory ideas, but her symptoms were primarily the disorganization of thoughts that had been residual symptoms previously.

Her husband reported that she was completely unable to care for the house or children and spent most of her time in idleness but seemed improved in that there were only rare occasions of excitement. It was impossible to take care of her at home since she refused to allow the housekeeper even to look after her children and he could not risk the patient's irresponsible care of the children. It was explained to the husband at the time of readmission that she would have another doctor and that if it were decided that nothing more could be offered except institutional care, Barbara might be later transferred to Jackson.

XIII
Brady Bunch Rewind

When I was in high school, the *Brady Bunch* television show and theme song permeated the airwaves and my consciousness. The Henke family had been living their own version of the program for several years already, though it looked little like the TV family. Sure, you had a woman with three lovely daughters and a man with three children of his own. But not all conflicts wrap up neatly in twenty-six minutes. There were obvious fallacies in the Hollywood example of merged families, but the expectations it created were troublesome. Maybe it was just that we didn't have an Alice to keep us in stitches and to deflect tension, but the on-air vision of blended households was simplistic and overly saccharine. Reality was sometimes disappointing by comparison.

Even though I now had a living, breathing mother in residence in the form of my stepmother Ruby, I continued to study mothers for clues to ideal motherhood. I dismissed the Carol Brady example as unrealistic, while clinging to my own overblown expectations. By this time, I'd analyzed mothers in the books I read, where I imagined myself as their daughter. Mrs. March, or "Marmee ," in *Little Women* had boundless patience and loving empathy for her four daughters. *Pride and Prejudice's* Mrs. Bennett was foolish and vain, but beneath all her worrying and conniving was genuine concern for her daughters' welfare.

None of these images fit the relationship I had with Mom. I'd learned "womanly" arts from her, but I resisted wholesale acceptance of her mothering. We often had different values. Reading fiction was one of my greatest joys, but Mom considered reading for enjoyment wasted time. My introverted nature led me to quieter pursuits, and spending time alone seemed odd or antisocial to the rest of the family.

The anonymity at LaGrange Senior High was as welcome as my transition from elementary to junior high school had been. It represented a convergence of students from several feeder schools, many of whom didn't know each other any better than I did. I was one of the crowd again, instead of the "new girl" at school. High school let me reinvent myself.

By that time, I was still adjusting to our new neighborhood, where we didn't really know any of the neighbors, but I'd become familiar with the school bus routine. My brother, Jon, graduated and went to Louisiana State University in Baton Rouge. My sister, Sue, soon found her own friends to drive her to school, leaving Yvonne and me to our own devices. Having at least one sister with me gave me some protection from the need to choose an appropriate bus seat. By myself? Near the front? Out of sight in the back? With the cute boy who lived the next street over? This is where I refined my aura of nonchalance. *Never let them see you care.*

I focused on my schoolwork, made good grades, and didn't cause trouble. Becoming inducted into the National Honor Society and taking part in a high school sorority club that focused on community service provided some social interaction. I made a few friends and was satisfied to be invisible to the rest of the student body. Yvonne, the extrovert, had joined the Gatorettes spirit marching group, where her active social life created lasting friendships. That just wasn't me.

Meanwhile, fitting into a new home life was challenging. I missed my father, who'd been wholly present for me and my siblings until he remarried. My biological siblings, Karen and Jon, were relieved to have someone they could call Mom, and I was too, but Jon and Karen soon left home—and me—behind. My new sisters, likewise, called my father "Dad," but perhaps they resented his role, too. We appeared to be a happily merged family—our own version of the Brady Bunch.

When I was in high school, my father delivered conflicting perceptions about who I might become. Proud of my interest in science and experimentation,

Dad once said, "You can be anything you want to be." I'd been debating my course selections for the next school year, and while he wasn't heavy-handed in his advice, he encouraged me toward the special chemistry class my high school offered. Over the next forty or fifty years, maybe to test his hypothesis, I tried on a lot of occupations to see how they fit. Most of them were related to science: medical technologist, biomedical research tech, science writer, science teacher, and college-level bioscience outreach coordinator. Each of my roles taught me something beyond what my father had, not the least of which was how little it can take to inspire a child; a simple chemistry set, and a few words of encouragement placed me on a career path that took profound but rewarding twists and turns.

Medical technology taught me the rewards of exploration and discovery if I'm patient and pay attention to each step. Biomedical research provided a chance to use creativity and problem-solving to develop innovative scientific procedures. My lab experiences and graduate-level journalism degree helped me translate science concepts into clear and comprehensible text for different audiences. Later in my career, all these skills culminated in teaching and encouraging older students toward their own journeys in education or science. Every one of these undertakings taught me the value of an open mind.

Around the same time he'd encouraged me

to achieve what I was capable of, Dad uttered a disturbing, contradictory message. In 1967, I signed up to join an inspirational choir group at our school called "Up With People." It proved challenging, but it was a challenge of inconvenience. I wasn't a talented musician, as my brief failed career as a sixth-grade clarinetist proved. Progress in playing an instrument or in singing with a choir demanded that I actually attend the practice sessions. Practicing what you're not good at can be hard on your self-esteem. After a few rehearsals, I decided not to expose myself to the humiliation any longer. When I announced I wouldn't take part in the choir anymore, Dad voiced his disappointment this way: "You're just like your mother. You never finish anything."

At fifteen, and considering the mother whose genes I possessed, one thing I did not want to be was like the mother I was born to. This was one puzzle piece I would've gladly lost. Dad was likely referring to Mother's false starts at sewing clothing and not the likelihood of my inheriting schizophrenia, but I couldn't unhear his words. I took up sewing during high school, with my stepmother's guidance, and made it my mission to finish everything I started. Fifty-plus years later, I'm barely able to return a library book before reading to the end, even if I hate it. In fact, I won't begin anything I don't believe I can finish. It means I'm dependable, but I can also be obsessive about fulfilling promises. Every positive quality can be carried too far.

When Dad likened me to my mother, it seemed like both a warning and a prediction. I'd done a little research, and though the Frieda Fromm-Reichmann theory that an unbalanced (schizophrenogenic) mother caused schizophrenia was being dismantled in the late 60s, it was also clear that genetics played a role. Neither possibility comforted me. Dad might have saved me from a schizophrenogenic mother's influence, but he couldn't save me from her genes.

That same year, a new family moved in next door on Ashland Street. Their daughter was near Sue's age, and a year older than me. Julia was the youngest of the three Crawford children. Her older, married sister lived in Arkansas, where the family had moved from, but her brother was serving in Việt Nam. I always felt a sense of fearful sadness in their home, where pictures of the Crawford's son hung on the wall in his military uniform. I suppose they weren't sure they'd ever see him again. Julia suffered from a serious kidney disease called glomerulonephritis, which made her vulnerable to infection. LaGrange Senior High's campus teemed with sweaty, pubescent teenagers; it rivaled a foul-smelling Petri dish for disease transmission. On her doctor's advice, she enrolled but did her lessons at home.

Because they were in the same grade, Julia and Sue struck up a friendship, but she and I also had a lot in common. Julia was a poet, and I was an aspiring writer. We sometimes compared our writing and shared similar poetic sensibilities. We also enjoyed divining our fates by questioning the Ouija "talking" board. I don't even remember whose board it was, but I recall several sessions in which we laughed over the ridiculous answers it spelled out. In response to our questions, the heart-shaped game piece glided to the letters or words printed on the board to give us answers. We were convinced we were talking to otherworldly spirits.

Not all answers were laughing matters, though. On one occasion, I asked who we were speaking to.

"B-o-n-n-i-e," I said, as each letter was revealed in the little round window. "Hmm. I don't know anyone named Bonnie. How old are you?" When the answer was 43, I was a little spooked. "When did you die?" The answers matched the age and year of my mother Bobbie's death.

"Let's see how long *we'll* live," Julia said.

I'm not certain today of the exact date revealed, but I would recall later that Julia's question was answered with a February day the following year. At that point, we became disenchanted with the Ouija board. We suspected the truth about who actually controlled the movement of our fingers—our subconscious impulses—yet we weren't confident how much we could really predict our futures. Having both experienced the deaths of family members, ideas about our own deaths were intriguing, but we preferred to think of other things.

I think Julia felt some responsibility for her parents' well-being. She was the only child left at home and they arranged their lives to protect her fragile health. Perhaps she felt her condition was a burden on them. She tried not to worry them, but she had an independent streak. We sometimes snuck out of one home or the other at night while our parents slept.

Day 'n Night Grocery, a few blocks from our houses, was notorious for selling cigarettes and alcohol to underage minors. I don't remember who bought them, but Julia and I shared a pack of Lucky Strikes, which we took turns concealing in our bedrooms.

On one occasion, we hopped the fence into the backyard of a vacant house for sale across the street from hers to smoke by the swimming pool. It was calm there, under the summer night sky. That the filled and forgotten pool had given over to brown sediment and a film of green slime didn't daunt us. As long as we kept our gaze from the dead frog floating in it, we could light up and pretend to live the lives of sophisticated, independent women, albeit life in which the cloud of cigarette smoke induced coughing fits. Another house for sale down the block had an unlocked gate leading to a courtyard we sneaked into for smokes a time or two. Besides not enjoying the coughing and sore throats, I think I was cautious about becoming addicted to tobacco as my mother had been and which my father still was. We were unaware of any aroused suspicions.

"My dad smelled smoke on my shirt," Julia said one day with some alarm.

"Oh no! What did you tell him?"

"I didn't have to say anything. Mom reminded him that your dad smokes cigars, and she thought

I'd probably just been over at your house while he was smoking."

The Lucky Strikes were shoved into the back of Julia's dresser drawer, and we were both relieved. Neither of us admitted we didn't enjoy smoking them.

Near the end of February in my junior year, Julia contracted spinal meningitis. We weren't allowed to visit her and knew that her situation was dire. Sue and I took preventive antibiotics and waited. Within days, Julia died. Perhaps it was simply a case of imaginative remembering, but I was convinced that day was the exact answer she'd gotten from our Ouija board session. No one else believed my assertion that Julia had predicted the date of her death, so after a couple of mentions were shrugged off, I shut up about it. While I now wonder if I forced the actual date to fit my memory, it isn't important. It gave me some small comfort to think Julia might have prepared mentally for her death.

While my mother had died the previous year, I hadn't really known her. This was different. This was the first death of someone I cared deeply for. However, per my typical reactions, I pretended to feel nothing, which troubled my sister Sue. At the funeral home on the evening of the viewing, I was there physically but not emotionally. When I took refuge in the bathroom, Sue followed me.

"You haven't cried," she said. I'd lost my mother years before she died and didn't grieve her death; Sue had experienced the sudden loss of her father and understood the value of tears. "You need to cry."

As soon as she put her arms around me, I broke down and sobbed until my body stopped shuddering. While I was a master at controlling my emotions when confronted with pain or disappointment, I dissolved in the face of such kindness. I'd been overcome with emotion the day President Kennedy was killed and remember bawling when I related the news to my father. This was my first taste of *personal* grief. I'd loved Julia. I hadn't shed a tear when my mother died and didn't recognize the depth of emotion that lurked behind my ironclad flood gates.

Mrs. Crawford gave Sue and me each a photocopied booklet of Julia's poetry called "Reflections" after she died, most of which she hadn't shared with me. The elegance of our late friend, the poet, touched me. I still smile at the words of one brief untitled poem:

When I am old—past twenty-four
Two things I want; no less, no more;
Maturity enough to be content
And wealth enough to pay the rent.

Julia never reached the old age of twenty-four, though, I think at sixteen, she'd learned to be content with the restrictions placed on her by her illness. Not long after Julia's death, the Crawfords moved back to Arkansas to be near their remaining daughter. I often wondered if they found peace.

I also wondered what her mother thought about the half-full pack of Lucky Strikes in Julia's dresser drawer.

A year later, when I was sixteen and my sister Sue was eighteen, our parents invited a large group of friends to our home for a New Year's Eve party. Sue and I arranged a double date out of the house that evening, which our parents appreciated so they could enjoy their friends without us. Yvonne was out of the house as well, perhaps with the boyfriend she eventually married.

None of the four of us had much alcohol tolerance; one drink is still my usual limit. In keeping with the holiday spirit, though, one of the boys brought alcohol along that evening. When the bottle of liquor was gone, I was the only one still sober. Therefore, I ended up the designated driver, fumbling my date's standard shift car along a route that seemed as tricky as an obstacle course. My three passengers attempted not to pass out or throw up in the car. Given the lurching at each transfer of my foot from the clutch to the brake or accelerator, this still amazes me. I stalled the car after almost every stop sign or stoplight. If I'd been a little smarter, I would've found someplace quiet to let them sleep it off. A staunch rule follower then and now, I was determined to get home before our stated curfew.

Our parents weren't prepared for our descent on their party. Our dates passed out on the living room floor almost as soon as we entered the house around midnight, and Sue made a beeline for her bedroom with a short, heaving stop in the bathroom.

"Jan made me do it," she accused, with a finger pointed in my direction, before she disappeared down the hall.

"There's a couple of frogs on your floor," a guest reported to Mom in the kitchen. The slurred "Happy New Year" one boy greeted party guests with as he fell to the floor hadn't been a proper introduction.

Mom called her oldest daughter Chris and son-in-law Ben to come take the two drunkards home to sleep it off on their sofa bed. The next morning, Sue clung to my side like Velcro on flannel, afraid of the reprimand she expected. Instead, Dad sat us down together to deliver his judgment, in his typical, calm and quiet style. "The next time you two decide to drink, do it at home," he said. While Sue might well have gotten a private earful from her mother, nothing else was said in my hearing.

During the summer before my senior year in 1969, I qualified for the Early Enrollment program at McNeese State University just a mile from our home. I enrolled in Freshman English and World History. Being a college coed at not-yet-seventeen was an intoxicating experience, though not literally. A couple of my classmates enrolled as well, and we spent afternoons reveling in our newfound freedom and cementing our friendships. We met some nice young college men who paid us attention and invited us to a few fraternity parties, which I didn't enjoy. Maybe it was because of the disastrous New Year's Eve party, but getting tipsy and losing control of my faculties wasn't much fun.

Sitting in the row behind me in English class was another high school student from Lake Charles High. I'd met him at one of my friend Janet's eighth-grade parties, where there were rock and roll 45s on the turntable and dancing on her garage floor. She had a crush on this boy named Tim Airhart from her Methodist youth group. I took particular note of him at the party so I could commiserate with her over his apparent lack of interest. I thought he was cute, but I had little interaction with him, and we never danced. He didn't know I existed until he took a seat behind me at McNeese.

Tim's red brown hair was long and sleek, as was the style in the Beatles era. He was tall and slim, with a smattering of freckles across his nose. He said little in class, and I didn't either, but I noticed a great deal more than I pretended. Instead, I played it cool, which was my teenage superpower. I was "Miss Henke" and he was "Mr. Airhart" to our professor. English was my best subject, but I don't remember any content from the semester. The cute guy behind me distracted me, so I noticed little else. A couple of times after class, Tim smiled and spoke to me, and I did likewise. I knew he was Janet's long ago crush while also knowing full well that he didn't recognize me. I found it awkward to flirt with a boy I hoped would notice me. Flirting was not my superpower.

The following April, a month before high school graduation, Tim and I met again. This time in the parking lot of a local hangout called Sam's Italian Village. Tim and his friend had just arrived, and my friend Anne and I were headed to her car. They'd ejected us from the bar after we paid for drinks we weren't legally old enough to purchase or consume; they didn't check our IDs until they took our money. Technically, Anne was old enough, but I was still seventeen and underage. She was kind enough to leave when I did.

"Miss Henke!" I hadn't seen Tim until I heard him call my name.

"Mr. Airhart!" I thought he was joking with me by using the formality our professor had insisted on, but he simply didn't know my first name.

After introducing each other to our friends, we decided to all get into Tim's car and go for a drive. We ended up at his friend's lake house for much of the evening.

The next couple of hours were a little surreal. This was a boy I'd been interested in, but who I thought wasn't interested in me. Within minutes, though, it was clear I'd been wrong. Even better, I found I could talk about things I cared about. I could be my geeky, awkward self, and he didn't seem turned off. We talked for hours and could've talked more, but Anne wanted to go home. She didn't think Tim's friend was her soulmate, and she was too busy fighting him off to know if they had anything in common. I'd been so engaged with soul baring and a good bit of kissing that I'd neglected to notice Anne's panicked attempts to keep her clothes on.

When we got back to the Burger Chef where Anne had parked her car, her boyfriend was staked out next to it. After an ugly scene, Tim and his friend drove me home, leaving Anne to work things out with Manuel. He forbade her to speak to me again, which saddened me. I didn't have so many friends I could easily lose one. Afterward, Tim and I became inseparable, and I viewed the whole incident, in spite of the unfortunate end, as more than simple chance; it seemed an instance of divine intervention.

On one of our next encounters, Tim softly kissed my eyelids, one after the other, and asked if I knew what it meant when someone kissed your eyes. When I shook my head, he said, "it means they love you." I'd felt the weak knees and stomach butterflies while reading romantic novels, but I'd never been the heroine of my own story and still don't think of myself as the romantic type. I was amazed he could see me for who I was—the child of an insane woman hiding behind the not-crazy persona I'd built to fit into a world where I was terrified of being inappropriate—and I could be loved in spite of it. It had been a long time since I'd felt loved for who I was.

The need to be loved is timeless and universal, so it's no surprise that this theme occupied at least one *Brady Bunch* television episode during its five-year run. In a 1969 show loosely based on a Cinderella theme, the youngest son ran away from home, convinced his family didn't love him. His stepmother sprang into action to save the day. Within a half hour, the Bradys had achieved resolution and their happily ever after. Not so in real life.

In my blended family, as opposed to the Brady family, the children had parents who were no longer living but whose presence pervaded thoughts and memories. In the television series, no parents or former spouses were ever mentioned, as though the six children had each sprung from a single parent. The Brady daughters adopted their stepfather's name, granting them an immediate place in the merged family. In our case, most peers didn't know my Lundgren sisters and I were family. While Mom and Dad and I carried the same last name, I felt like an intruder in their union. Four years later, on an April evening in 1970, when I was unceremoniously thrown out of a bar and into a chance relationship, I finally felt I belonged with someone.

Southeast Louisiana Hospital
Henke, Barbara
Hospital Number 201

Selected Psychiatric Notes

January 11, 1956:

When checking the bedside table, two doses of medication were found wrapped in Kleenex in her purse. Looked partly melted.

June 19, 1956:

Patient upset walking up and down, let out one scream, then quieted down. Came and sat in dayroom with clothing on. Was offered a pair of pajamas but wouldn't put them on.

July 1, 1956:

Patient did not swallow medication. I followed her; she spit it in her hand. Thelma H. was standing by her and asked her to take it. She slapped Thelma in the mouth with the pills in her hand and said, "You take them." I got her to take the Thorazine when I told her that I would have to give it in a shot if she didn't.

July 20, 1956:

Patient attacked volunteer worker as she

was taking patient on pass to shop. Slapped and pulled her hair. Also tore volunteer worker's dress. When attendants and Helen M. went in there, she turned on them. Slapped M. and pulled her hair. Patient had a wild look in eyes. Patient was held down until help came and then was taken to C-1.

XIV
God in Her Image

One Sunday in 1978, when I was the mother of two, Lois Bekkerus pulled me aside. Lois was a matriarch of St. Paul Lutheran Church and a mainstay in my Christian education. She sidled up to me just after Sunday School ended and whispered in my ear, "we enjoyed having Marc for Sunday School this morning."

"What?" I was confused. Lois taught the confirmand class—seventh and eighth graders preparing for their first communions and confirmations as adult members of the church. We sent our son Marc off to the fellowship hall and education building for his own second-grade class that morning as usual.

Lois beamed and shrugged. "He sat in on our

class this morning, I guess. I didn't notice him at first. About halfway through the lesson, I saw his head pop up several rows behind the rest of the class."

I still didn't understand, "What was he doing there?"

Lois's head skewed to one side and her look said, come on. Really?

"Oh." Marc skipped Sunday School that day and picked what he considered a safe place to hide. He hadn't counted on crashing another class. "I'm sorry," I said, but Lois waved away my apology.

"I didn't let on I'd seen him," she said, "I just kept on with the catechism lesson. Before long, he sat up straight and listened, quiet as can be." She chuckled. "He might've been my best student today."

I had to laugh with her. "Thanks for letting me know." It was just like this woman I'd known for so long, this woman I'd grown up in the church with, this woman who'd known me since I was even younger than Marc was. She'd been my Sunday School teacher off and on for years, and it seemed fateful that she was now teaching my son.

Lois had spent a long career as a special education teacher in her daughter Becky's classes, as well as our nephew Jason's class years later. She was a church fixture for years, doing whatever needed doing. There were potluck dinners to set up, dishes to wash afterwards, bathrooms and floors to clean, worship services to plan, and youngsters to be taught and molded by her patient and caring example.

Lois was only one of the women who shepherded

me throughout my youth and young adulthood with dedication and patience. Dad was a devout Lutheran, like his parents and grandparents before him. Taking part in church functions was a given for my siblings and me. The bonus, tucked inside the expectation to be active in the life of our church, was the love and care I received from the many church women who stood in as mothers.

There was Kathleen, a stalwart teacher and meal preparer, whose husband Floyd put a one-dollar bill in the offering plate every Sunday until the day he died. "Our time is our offering," he insisted. My father took over the post as financial secretary for the congregation after my grandfather died in 1984, leaving the post vacant. Dad used to shake his head at Floyd's stubbornness, but he appreciated the couple's hard work and commitment. The last time I saw Kathleen was at Mom's memorial service in 2018. She was frail and shrunken, but her smile and her hug were as welcoming as they'd ever been.

There was Ampie, about whose husband I'd hear murmurs from time to time, "Charlie's gone off on his own again." She and her three children would show up without him one Sunday, and heads would shake in sympathy for poor Ampie. Charlie once formed his own church and called the congregation the River Rats. We didn't see him for a year or two, then he'd come back—but only until his next snit. The epitome of patience, Ampie pursed her lips and continued on as though nothing were amiss, setting out sandwiches for a reception or arranging flowers for the altar without a word about her husband.

Mae, a single mom with a joyful laugh and infectious sense of humor, sponsored youth group activities, ferrying kids from Lake Charles east to New Orleans or west to Texas for youth group retreats and other events. One pastor's wife called on me to babysit for their young daughter a few times while she busied herself in another room with their infant son. I was quite young and suspect now she was the one babysitting me. "You're so good with Rebecca," she'd say with a great big hug when Dad picked me up. I felt proud to be helpful.

Pastors came and went from our church. As a fledgling congregation, we drew a lot of new seminary graduates who served a few years until they got some parish experience and moved on to larger churches. During the twenty-six years I was a member of St. Paul Lutheran Church, a host of different pastors officiated at my life's most critical events: baptisms, confirmations, weddings, and memorial or funeral services. Pastor Eckhart officiated at my mother's funeral in 1966, and because Dad didn't own a cemetery plot, the pastor donated the space his parents had purchased next to theirs and intended for his use one day. Consequently, my mother is buried apart from my father, who we buried next to his parents in a cemetery across town. My stepmother Ruby's ashes were interred in the same cemetery a few years ago, across the lawn from both husbands she'd lost.

Through my early years and beyond, I viewed the people of St. Paul as family and the church as home. For much of my youth, church was the only place I felt I belonged. At my sister Karen's memorial service in 2019, most of the women who'd guided and cared for me through the years were gone, but a few of their children were there, and regardless of who is serving the parish as pastor from one year to the next, St. Paul is a permanent feature in my memory. My childhood homes are sheltering strangers now, but the sanctuary and fellowship hall are as familiar to me as the freckle on the inside of my right wrist or the prayer I've repeated at daily meals since I was a child. Until Hurricane Laura destroyed the "new" sanctuary in 2020—sparing the wood altar my grandfather had constructed for its dedication in 1974—the buildings changed little in almost fifty years.

While attending worship, singing in the choir, or visiting with friends during or after youth or congregational activities, I developed a deep recognition of the God who encompassed it all, and whose face resembled the ones I worshiped with and learned from. I felt the presence of God more keenly than that of my mother who lived hours away and internalized the concept of God as an all-loving presence. The quiet examples I saw of trusted adults who loved this God seeped into my soul. During times of turmoil in my teenage years, when I contemplated taking my life as an end to sorrow over feeling that I didn't belong where I was placed, I called on God for strength and comfort, and they were sufficient.

I don't remember a time when I wasn't conscious of God. Dad didn't discuss faith with us—his *or* ours—although he brought my brother, my sister, and me to St. Paul every week without fail. We prayed memorized prayers at mealtimes and at bedtime when I was young, and we were all three baptized and confirmed in the Lutheran faith. Without sermonizing, Dad showed us that the church was a valuable place to be, that the congregation we belonged to was our family.

Year after year, I was immersed in Lutheran liturgical tradition and Lutheran Protestant perspectives on scripture. Tim and I still recite Martin Luther's table prayer at most meals. I can sing all three verses of the hymn "This is My Father's World," and I can say the Apostles Creed and the Words of Institution without looking at the text. Fragments of Luther's Small Catechism are indelibly etched in my memory. *This is most certainly true.*

Something else happened while I was prodding immature brain cells toward comprehension of the Holy Trinity. There was a silent heart seeking I wasn't aware of. Henry David Thoreau once said, "Nature abhors a vacuum, and if I can only walk with sufficient carelessness, I am sure to be filled." My young mind was so crammed full of void and so eager to erase it that it fused two concepts in my consciousness. I suppose by their bumping against each other through all that emptiness, my understandings of a mother and of the One True God merged.

My mother was the most important person absent from my life while God was omnipresent. I was taught that God was love, pure and unqualified; I assumed mothers were the same. When I needed the solace of a tender touch, it was God's hand I imagined against my cheek. When I imagined myself too old for the ceremonial tucking in at bedtime, I shrugged off Dad's company, but I invited the Divine Comforter to rest companionably on the edge of my bed and share my growing-girl secrets.

God became a mother to me as no one else could. She came the night I lay on tear-soaked pillow, heartsore from learning to live with a new sister who had wounded me in her own struggle to learn to live with me. "What am I supposed to do?" I cried to Mother God between angry sobs. I felt a gentle nudge toward a more loving attitude, as a mother might have encouraged.

In the following years, there were many occasions in which I recognized blessings and comforts as divine consolations when I needed them most. When our daughter Kelly was an infant, she developed croup, which constricted her breathing passages and left her to inhale as if through pinholes. Between gasps, she alternately barked a cough and sobbed. My heart lurched in fear at each ragged attempt to inhale—it seemed each one might be her last. Later, while I lay curled on the stiff vinyl mattress on its squeaky wire frame in her hospital room, I listened to her raspy breath under the dome of her oxygen tent. The injections and inhalations had begun their work, and I trusted they would continue to soothe and relax swollen tissues. The Mother Who Waits waited with me during the dark, anxious night, as though soothing my brow with warm, fragranced hands and whispers of care.

Mother God continued her vigil through the years

of my children's growing, through seasons of sorrow and joy. She was present through all the transitions as well: deaths of those I loved, my children's weddings, and the births of my three grandchildren. I called on this ever-present spirit named God to fill the void my mother had left. I don't think I'm alone in creating a God in an image that fulfills my needs.

At a training session on domestic violence I attended several years ago, one speaker—a theology professor from a local seminary—commented that it isn't helpful to discuss biblical theology with domestic violence perpetrators, who are overwhelmingly male. Some know the words of scripture better than theologians. They use them to batter the weaker members of their family with a sense of righteous will, as though God commands them to make their wives, their property, submit by any means necessary. What's more helpful is knowing we all see the Bible as communication from or about God. "How we interpret the words depends on who we believe God is." Changing one's interpretation of what's read can only happen if one changes his or her image of God. And mine has endured many, many changes in perspective. Over the years, I've sought texts on feminist theology, contemplative prayer, historical accounts of the mystics, books by Jesus Seminar scholars, skeptics, and monks. I enjoy being both edified and provoked; I'd rather be labeled an atheist than a narrow-minded Christian.

If I believe God is a god of power and might, I can read in the words of scripture a command to subdue and conquer and believe I have license to do the same. If I believe God is as nurturing and sustaining as a mother, I read an admonition to protect her creation and her beloved creatures. Maybe both images of God are wrong. Or they're both right. At best, they're both incomplete. At the least, my mental and emotional melding of Mother and God created impossible expectations for any human to fill. Neither Ruby nor I could, certainly. That didn't stop me from using a Mother-God gauge to measure our effectiveness, though.

In 2019, we traveled back to Lake Charles and St. Paul Lutheran for my sister Karen's memorial service after her sudden death following a stroke, and I learned that Lois Bekkerus had also died, a week before Karen, at age 98. Several years earlier, Lois and Becky had donated the home in Lake Charles they'd lived in for over forty years to the church as a parsonage and moved to a retirement community in Anaheim, California. Their assisted living apartment was in a community administered by the national Lutheran (ELCA) church. It had been a sudden and seemingly impulsive move; they had no family or friends in California, no family left anywhere. But Lois's former husband had left them enough means to live a modest life in a continuum of care facility, and it seemed another act of faith for Lois to put herself and her daughter in their hands. She trusted the church to care for Becky after she was gone. Even after death, this woman who had influenced my developing faith life still had a lesson to teach me. She and the other women in the church of my youth, as well as fellow church members in the years after, shaped my character as surely as any mother might have.

Southeast Louisiana Hospital
Henke, Barbara
Hospital Number 201

Selected Psychiatric Notes

August 14, 1956:

At 2:15 a.m. in bedroom had one seizure. Preliminary signs:

Patient gave one loud scream. Patient's body was found jumping and foaming from mouth. Her eyes were closed. Respiration 24. No cyanosis noted. Pulse was found strong, also unconscious. Duration of seizure lasted for ten minutes.

August 28, 1956:

Barbara will not stop smoking in bed. Has been told over and over. Had to get her out of bed with cig three or four times. Patients complain of her smoking in bed.

September 13, 1956:

7:25 am. Screaming and walking in day room in very rapid circles. Seems very confused. Says, "Such brutality. My legs are firing up. How long will this last?" Pulling up her skirt and fanning leg. To Lodge on C-1 until she quiets down.

September 27, 1956:

Had a seizure lasted about 5 minutes.

September 28, 1956:

Patient had a seizure lasted 10 minutes. Body was stiff. Patient was on her bed.

XV
Karen

"You're a woman now!" Karen said and threw her arms around me.

When she let me go, I regarded her with suspicion. She must be crazy. I grunted my response. At twelve, I didn't *want* to be a woman—not if it came with blood spots in my underwear. And not with this uneasy feeling in my midsection.

"What do I do now?"

Karen rustled around in our bathroom closet and dug deep into the back to pull out a box of Kotex. "You'll need these," she said and handed me a pad, an elastic band with metal fastener-thingies dangling from it, and a pamphlet.

"What am I supposed to do with this?" I said, holding up the belt.

"Read the instructions," Karen said, pointing to the small booklet. She grinned, patted my shoulder, and left me alone in the bathroom.

Being a woman wasn't appealing when it included this odd contraption. I followed the instructions for slipping the Kotex tails into place on the belt and positioned it as directed between my legs, thoroughly disgusted. When I read the pamphlet, circa 1964, I knew where Karen had gotten her script. It began with the bold heading: "You're a Young Lady Now!" Neither the smiling girl with her cuffed denim jeans, bobby socks, and pigtails nor the image in the mirror of her more mature, womanly self with a dress and fashionable, bow-topped hair looked anything like me.

It felt like the pad hidden beneath my clothes was visible, and I couldn't stop fidgeting with it or walking like a cowboy with boot spurs to keep it from shifting to one side. The topic of menstruation and periods popped up in whispered conversations with my sixth-grade classmates, but we hadn't talked about details. Nobody mentioned the paraphernalia required. I wondered why I'd never noticed Karen becoming a "young lady." Where had she learned what to do when it happened to her? Who had taught her?

Karen was the extrovert to my introvert and never seemed hesitant to jump into situations that I held back from. She could be a badass in getting things done right. If you needed someone to call the plumber or the cardiologist and get a bill straightened out, she was your go-to. She could cuss the paint off walls when needed, but she was also devoutly spiritual and compassionate, caring deeply for strays—both human and animal. She devoted much of her energy to their rescue. Like me, she'd learned to keep her personal life separate from her school activities.

After plunging into drama productions in high school, beginning with *Bye Bye Birdie*, Karen discovered her true home; she was in love with music and musical plays. She had the soundtrack album from the 1961 *West Side Story* movie and played it so often I've still got some lyrics memorized. Her favorite numbers were "Maria" and "I Feel Pretty." I can almost hear her singing them now, in her lilting soprano. I loved listening to her, entranced by the joy it brought her, but hung back to avoid intrusion into her improvised one-woman dance parties. I think she enjoyed having an audience.

Perhaps Karen resented the responsibility of being the older sister in a home in which there was a void where a mother should have been. She'd lost her mother too. Our housekeepers were kind, but not affectionate, and the three of us were happy enough in their presence. Maybe somewhere deep inside, Karen remembered a mother who doted on her as a much-loved first daughter. I'd like to think this was among her memories, even if she wasn't aware of it. Expressed or not, and despite her sometimes strained tolerance of a younger sister who annoyed her, I never doubted my sister wanted the best for me.

Karen and I never brawled, as sisters often do, though there were occasional disagreements, and she could sometimes be bossy. Karen, Jon, and I often played the Monopoly board game, but only by Karen's rules: she could purchase the orange properties no matter who landed on them. Always the banker, she would offer a loan if we ran short, as long as we signed the bank note she created. I accepted her rules and my station as her underling, and she persisted in introducing me to others as her baby sister: her friends and acquaintances, clerks at retail shops, and her ICU nurses when we were both in our sixties. There were enough physical similarities that we were recognized as kin, but Karen had a different build. Where Jon and I were taller and leaner, Karen was shorter and broad-shouldered, looking more like my father's sister than our mother, but there were resemblances. It was her care for me that best characterized our relationship as sisters.

Once, when I was fifteen, the year after our father's remarriage to Ruby, I asked if my longtime friend Janet could spend the night. My father and stepmother refused because they didn't feel there was room. I groused my disappointment to Karen, who was married to her first husband, Don. She invited me and Janet to spend the night on their living room sleeper sofa. In recognition of our boundary-testing teenaged tendencies, she gave us each one can of beer and one cigarette and went to bed. "Just don't leave the house," she said.

As she should have expected, we repaid her misplaced trust by consuming our beers then sneaking out of the house to embellish with toilet paper the home of a boy I had a crush on across town. When the police car pulled up in Karen's driveway at around 3 am, Janet and I in tow, she took us in with pursed lips and sent us to bed. She never mentioned our delinquency after that day and never told our parents.

A few short years later, I married and soon had two children. Tim and I moved to Texas, where I busied myself with parenting and professional pursuits, Ping-Ponging between Texas and Oklahoma with Tim's job transfers for nearly forty years. Karen had meanwhile found her life's passion as the coordinator of the Newspaper in Education program at the local newspaper. We communicated, but irregularly. When Karen's worsening health forced her departure from the *Lake Charles American Press*, we both found time for telephone calls a couple of times a week. Reconnecting was a "coming home" of sorts. Ours was a relationship in which I could share anything I cared to. My sister knew me better than anyone else ever has or will, and she loved me still.

When Karen had shoulder surgery in 2008, I spent a week at her home helping her recover. Again, in the summer of 2016, I drove from our home in Oklahoma to Lake Charles to assist her after hip replacement, which didn't go as planned. Complications landed her in ICU, near death for weeks. Never good, her health deteriorated for the decade prior to her death. She'd suffered asthma and potentially fatal food allergies when she was young and, in later years, cascading skeletal or joint problems because of the many years of daily steroid injections used to treat the childhood maladies. Karen had undergone two complete sets of knee replacements, one hip replacement, and two reverse shoulder replacements. She had misaligned hips and Charcot foot deformity—known as rocker-bottom feet—that caused constant pain when walking. Her diabetes, frequent bouts of bronchitis, dangerously low kidney function, and persistent asthma had taken their toll.

Despite these challenges, Karen refused to let pain stop her from doing what she wanted to do as long as she could move her body and rotate her Honda's steering wheel. While she might misjudge the distance between her bumper and other cars, there were no major incidents. At seventy-one, she was more active with her disabilities than many fifty-year-olds in good health. She was that stubborn, and some family members (my husband, for instance) would say I inherited the same stubborn streak. To be honest, I see it as an asset. I admired my sister's persistence, what our brother Jon affectionately calls "intransigence."

Her intransigence accounted for a bit of drama during one hospitalization for bronchitis-turned-pneumonia in February 2018. During one of the annual near-death experiences she suffered, Karen spent several days in ICU, much of the time not aware of her surroundings. One morning when I arrived in ICU, to my great surprise, she was sitting up, watching TV and talking with her nurse. It was a Rip Van Winkle awakening. They planned to move her to a regular floor as soon as a room was available. I happily agreed to pick up her iPad from her home and bring it to the hospital, at which point she requested the Wi-Fi password and began typing away.

A few days earlier, during the confusion of her ambulance ride and emergency room visit, her wallet was lost. In the meantime, Jon's wife Trudy had asked the bank to monitor the credit card accounts for fraudulent charges. Sometime later, Trudy returned from Texas to sit with Karen while I went home to Oklahoma. When Karen's discharge was imminent, Trudy learned of a credit card charge to QVC that occurred on a day that Karen was in ICU. She alerted me. "There's no way this charge could have been hers!" When Trudy told Karen about it, her reply was cavalier.

"Oh, that was me," Karen responded. "They featured a sale on the makeup I use. It was a great deal." Not even confinement to an ICU bed could keep my sister and her iPad from passing up a QVC deal!

In March 2019, Karen's second husband lost his battle with Alzheimer's after a two-year nursing home stay. Tim and I weren't able to make the trip to Lake Charles, but Karen and I talked every day before and after Dale's death about the plans she was making for his cremation and memorial service. I was finishing up a semester of teaching and had gotten permission to give my finals online during the week of our Oklahoma-to-Texas move the following month and didn't feel I could ask for more leave time.

"You don't need to come. I've got plenty of help," Karen assured me. But she was weary. I could hear the exhaustion in her voice as we talked each evening.

She perked up the day of Dale's service, though, delighted to see his former classmates and newspaper colleagues. He'd worked at the *American Press*, too, until he was diagnosed with Alzheimer's disease. People she hadn't seen in years came to pay respects. "It was like 'old home week.' It was wonderful to see everyone," she said the evening of the service. Many of Karen's friends who didn't know Dale came to give her love and support as well. The outpouring of care overwhelmed her. In an odd way, it was like being present at her own memorial service and became eerily predictive.

Karen was ferocious as a big sister and defender, and I appreciated that about her, but it didn't relate to my skewed concept of a mother as something of an eternal Madonna (not the "Material Girl"). I'd also never considered that her attitude toward Mother could be so different from mine. I assumed she longed for the mother we'd lost, as I had.

"Oh, I *hated* her. I wanted her gone so that we could have a real mother," Karen said.

It was late April, a few weeks after her husband's death and three days before the stroke that killed her. I'd asked, "What do you remember about the months our mother lived with us in 1958 and '59?" This was just before Mother got transported back to the state psychiatric hospital permanently. Those ten months were scary and unpredictable. I spent most of the time in-between Mother's weekly ECT sessions watching her with the laser focus of a dog staring at another dog gnawing a pork chop bone in case something might be tossed her way. A word or a smile would've satisfied me. Did she even know who I was? The intense scrutiny I leveled on my mother could give anyone the jitters. For a schizophrenic with paranoid tendencies, my neediness might well have challenged her fragile coping skills. If her pregnancy with me hadn't initiated a drift toward psychosis, this might well have. One more layer of self blame.

While Karen and I hadn't spoken a great deal about our mother in the previous decade, I thought she might have a more mature perspective of events, or at least more cohesive memories, and I was considering taking up my stalled memoir again after our move. Maybe what I wanted to ask was, "Am I like her?" but I didn't think she knew. I had sensed Karen harbored more resentment than I did, but I had no idea she was so bitter, over sixty years after Mother's death.

"Really?" I was puzzled. After a pause I said again, "*Really*?"

"I just hated her," she repeated, "I wanted a real mother."

"I was always looking for a mother too," I told her. I thought we'd each found what we needed in the people around us: teachers, neighbors, and women at church. We'd learned how to mother ourselves and to invent who we needed a mother to be.

"You may be right," she said, "I just know I didn't want the one we had."

Instead, we got a stepmother who took us on when we were 14, 17, and 19—no small feat. In many ways, Ruby came too late to be the mother we'd once hoped for.

In 1950, psychologist Erik Erikson described adolescence as a stage of psychosocial development between 12 – 18 years when youth are sorting out their identity in a process called individuation. In the earliest stages of development, a young child attaches to a trusted adult, usually a mother. Adolescents then experience a strong urge to separate from that adult several years later. For me, at the same time I'd gained a mother to which I might attach, I was simultaneously seeking my independent identity. No wonder I was conflicted.

At the height of the feminist movement, nearly a decade after I left home, psychotherapist Jane Flax redefined this dissonance as it applied to women. Her article appeared in a June 1978 issue of *Feminist Studies*. Flax theorized that mothers and daughters experience unique conflicts—animosity even—

because of their desires to nurture/be nurtured and to achieve autonomy. Daughters realize they're more like their mothers than their fathers, but they also rebel at being too much like her. "I'm turning into my mother!" is often the horrified response. Reading Flax's article, I recognize the desire I once felt for my stepmother to nurture and approve of me at the same time I was pushing her away. God knows Ruby's job was hard enough as it was with two adolescent daughters of her own, but then a third one entered the mix. I'm surprised any of us survived.

For a few days after our last phone conversation when I'd prodded my sister for memories and into the following week when I flew to New Orleans where they airlifted her after her stroke, I pondered what Karen told me. I mentioned it to my husband, a few close friends, and Trudy, who I joined in the ICU vigil. It was the first time I realized the depth of difference between her perspective and mine. Our brother, Jon, never spoke of Mother, and I suspected he didn't remember her fondly either, but I was unsure how he felt. It was a revelation that their feelings could be so different from mine. As the youngest, I'd been less affected by circumstances in some ways, less cognizant of our mother's both gradual and sudden departures from sanity. In other ways, I think my yearning for what I missed created a sense of loss that neither of my siblings felt.

"I'm surprised that she still seems to blame our

mother for the way her illness made her act," I told my husband.

"Don't judge," he said.

"I'm not judging; I'm just so surprised. After over sixty years, what she remembers best is the schizophrenia-crazed woman our mother became." What I'd wanted to know more than anything was who our mother was *before* schizophrenia. I'd accumulated any photograph or artifact I could get, but there were few. Asking questions seemed forbidden in a home where we never discussed my mother, never told family stories. Rules about *what must not be spoken aloud* are sometimes the easiest to enforce.

A few days after our phone conversation, at the annual Easter morning pancake breakfast at St. Paul Lutheran, a few yards from where our father had collapsed with a fatal heart attack in 1994, Karen had a stroke. Members of her St. Paul family surrounded her, one of them the hospice chaplain—the pastor's wife—who'd cared for Mom the year before. It was Robin who called for an ambulance and then called our sister Chris.

After I got the call about Karen's stroke, I was torn. Movers were coming to load our furniture and household goods for transport from Oklahoma to Texas ten days later. Most of the packing still awaited. When I got the news of her transfer to New Orleans, I hesitated. Life-and-death crises invariably choose the worst possible timing. Chris and her husband drove over from Lake Charles that night after returning from a vacation trip. Then our sister-in-law Trudy flew in from a vacation in Virginia the next day to meet Chris and send her home.

"You should go," Tim said, "I can finish the packing. Don't worry." When I hesitated, he said, as though I might have forgotten, "She's your sister."

Trudy said, "You don't need to come; you've got enough on your plate. Karen doesn't know I'm here, anyway."

But Karen was my sister.

I arrived late on Wednesday night and took a cab to meet Trudy at the hospital. She took me to ICU, where it was clear this hospitalization differed from the many before. Karen looked worse than ever—they'd entered her skull to drain the bleeding, and her head was swollen to the size of a soccer ball. They'd shaved half her head.

"She'll be furious if she wakes up and sees they only shaved half," Trudy said.

The next day, there was a conference with Karen's neurologic surgeon. She showed us the progression of MRIs from just after the stroke until the previous day. There had been the one surgery, in which they'd cauterized the primary artery feeding the left side of her brain, as it had bled and caused the initial stroke. By this time, it was unmistakable on film: the bleeding had not stopped. The artery was continuing to bleed, although more slowly, and the leaked blood put pressure on the surrounding brain tissue, causing more damage.

"We'd hoped cauterizing the artery would stop the bleeding, but it didn't," the doctor said, "We could try again, but going in again will damage even more tissue. In any case, I don't think they would approve the surgery." Since I'd just arrived, the doctor asked me to tell her what I knew of Karen's status to make sure I understood, and she seemed satisfied with my account of events as I'd learned them from both Chris and Trudy. I felt as though I were taking an oral exam.

I maintained composure until she said, "Tell me about Karen." It's simple kindnesses that bring tears. She asked what her life had been like. What did she care most about? We told her about Karen's love of literature, her love of learning, how she'd been passionate about her work in newspaper education.

Trudy related the hospitalizations in the past few years, each one seeming to be the last one. "We thought she was gone at least three times before. But she's tough. She always pulled through."

I felt myself trembling. "She would not want to live without language," I said through tears.

"Her language center is already destroyed," the doctor said gently, while handing me a tissue. "There's no chance we can restore it. None."

Trudy and I made the tough decision to discontinue life support, and after we signed consent, the plan was to pull the tracheal tube that afternoon. We called the family to make sure no one wanted to come and maybe to be assured we were doing the right thing. After the respiratory therapist extubated Karen, the nurse told us we could "love on her." They warned us she might stop breathing soon or that it might be hours. We stroked her arms and face. We told her we loved her; we reminded her she was well loved by all.

"You're the best big sister anyone could have," I told her.

About a half hour later, her breathing became more labored for a few minutes before it stopped. I'm not sure if she was aware of our presence or of the words we spoke in those last moments. Perhaps at least some part of her recognized she was not alone, that she'd joined our parents (all three of them), her two late husbands, and her best friends Sarah and Kathy on the other side. Comprehension of her passing had not yet made its way from my head to my heart; it was surreal.

This is what I remember about her last moments: Karen's hands were as warm as newly hatched chicks. After the respirator stopped hissing and her body shuddered with the effort of the last ragged breath, her hands still radiated the warmth of her laughter and the joy of her singing. Mine were as cold as stones, already contemplating loss.

This is what I wonder about her last moments: Is it a mercy she was spared the knowledge of her half-shaved head? Could she feel us there in the ICU, clutching her hands as though to hold her back from death? Did she know she'd been more than my big sister, that her care for me was everything I'd hoped for from a mother?

One item I rescued from the mess at Karen's home after her death was her Bible. This was after her husband's niece and the niece's husband—two of the human strays she'd taken in over the years—ransacked every cabinet, closet, and shelf to take what they could sell following her stroke. They had little use for her Bible. Karen had been teaching fifth- and sixth-grade Sunday School, and inside the zippered book bag were some lesson sheets. One was a job application for a hypothetical position as newspaper reporter for a church newsletter, as described in the curriculum they used. It asked her to name special people in her life. She listed her husband, my brother, and me. Beside "sister," it said, "know everything about each other and still love each other." She also wrote in the space that asked for something not everyone knew about her: "my brother, sister, and I were raised by our loving Lutheran father and the folks at St. Paul Lutheran Church; our mother was sick in the hospital." That bond of understanding and shared experience between us was strong, as strong as any mother and daughter experienced.

That we could love each other despite knowing each other so well was the truth, but it had still surprised me to realize how Karen viewed our mother and perhaps more so that I hadn't known it before. Why didn't she long for our mother as I did? I was fortunate to have an older sister to teach and protect me as a mother would've done; I'd leaned on her since childhood and had always been confident she would support me. Who did Karen have?

In the years since Karen's delivery of a stillborn daughter when she was twenty-one, I'd given little thought to the niece we'd never known, who'd arrived as still as a held breath in 1969. The baby's father died a few years later from complications of hemophilia, a devastating and often fatal disease their daughter Mary would have carried, as a female, but would not have suffered from herself. The pregnancy had occurred despite contraceptive use, and I'd always assumed her parents' relief at knowing the disease wouldn't be passed on. I wish I'd thought to ask Karen how she felt about never becoming a mother. She'd have been good at it.

A couple of weeks after Karen's death, I dreamed we were part of a large dinner gathering—perhaps a potluck or a banquet. When it was time to leave, we gathered our dishes and our family and headed to the car. Karen asked us to drop her off at church.

"We can take you home," I said.

"No. My friend Kathy is going to pick me up from there." Kathy was a longtime close friend of Karen's who'd died several months before. No one in my dream was chained to their mortality. We did as Karen asked and left her at the church to wait for Kathy to collect her.

The scene shifted to the huge multi-story atrium of a hotel lobby. We were waiting for Karen near the front door, and when I looked up to find her, I saw a long, polished ramp leading from the floor above to where we were standing. An eighteen-year-old Karen, free of the hip dysplasia and other painful body changes that had plagued her last twenty years, came charging down the ramp at breakneck speed—on roller skates. When she reached the bottom, she pivoted and stopped with outstretched arms and a flourish, one toe gliding across the gleaming floor with all the skill of a Roller Derby Queen. She turned to me with a proud grin, "Look at me!"

I still like to think of Karen in her afterlife as young, healthy, and strong, the way she appeared in my dream. She came of age during the 1960s, learning to value the underdog or the dispossessed and despising armed conflict of any kind. Her world view was formed by cultural icons like Woody Guthrie; Bob Dylan; and Peter, Paul, and Mary. I like to think of her in some time and space, singing along and boogying to the *Bye Bye Birdie* soundtrack or to Dylan's "Like a Rolling Stone," which played in the background during our last phone conversation. Heaven as only my sister could invent it.

Southeast Louisiana Hospital
Henke, Barbara
Hospital Number 201

Selected Psychiatric Notes

January 26, 1957:

Patient had another seizure. Lasted 5 min. When patent came to, she stated her right arm hurt. Patient did not fall or hit any object. She was throwing her arms and jumping up in bed when coming out of seizure. Nurse notified.

February 9, 1957:

Patient stated she wanted to go home to her husband and children. But the last time she was home they had a big fight and that was why her husband brought her back. Patient also said her husband wanted to split the family up. But she felt like she could be discharged and get a job and work and take care of her children.

February 9, 1957:

Barbara Henke was standing at nurse's station and Hanna M. came to the station to ask for a pack of Old Gold cigarettes and Barbara Henke hit Hanna M. on the head.

February 12, 1957:

Patient very upset. Came up to nurse's station door, crying, saying one of the girls came to her and asked her to have homosexual with her, and she asked the attendant what shall she tell them. She refused to tell the name of the girl because she did not want to get anybody in trouble.

XVI
Motherhood 101

He wouldn't stop crying. My infant son was in his crib in the next room. "Just go to sleep," I muttered from my bed, one summer afternoon in early 1972. I listened to the wailing through the pillow I'd pulled over my ears for another several minutes before I started to cry too. I think he stopped before I did.

No one warned me about days like these. Days when I arrived at the hospital at 6:00 a.m. and worked until 3:30 or 4:00. Days when I was on my feet all day and just wanted a few minutes of rest before the daily responsibilities of my new life as a wife and mother began. No one warned me that the joys of motherhood could be so rudely shattered by prolonged exhaustion and sleeplessness. Becoming a mother had seemed a reward for having survived a motherless childhood and for observing with fascination how other mothers managed their roles. Since no one else in my family or circle of friends had babies, and I'd had no one to model baby-tending skills, this meant studying strangers. Other moms kissed and hugged adorable little sprites in clean and stylish onesies with joyous enthusiasm; I eagerly awaited a similar state of euphoria. Fantasies die hard.

My own start at mothering was confusing. To be sure, there were minutes—whole hours, sometimes—when our child giggled his delight at a game of peekaboo while he sported his own clean and stylish onesie. But it wasn't easy to ignore his vomit stains on our bedspread or the poop that sometimes flowed out of his diaper edges, bubbled through the snaps on the crotch of said onesie, and slid down his adorable little chubby legs into his darling little child-size sneakers. Invariably, the stinky mess sliding the length of his legs occurred in the least convenient places: in the car on the way to visit friends who'd never met our handsome progeny, while waiting fourth in line at the grocery checkout of a swamped Kroger store on Saturday, or in the middle of a Sunday sermon. It was hard to pretend we were cool-headed, doting parents in the face of such reality. How did other mothers do it? I wondered. The scenarios we confronted hadn't ever presented themselves during the months of my pregnancy when I stared in near obsession at mothers interacting with their children in public places. I surmised they were more capable of preventing such crises or they weren't similarly fazed by mopping up shit with a spare onesie, the only clean item in the diaper bag.

I was nineteen when our son was born in 1971, and just barely so. When I missed first one period and then two, I made an appointment with a doctor whose name was familiar from my weekend job in the hospital laboratory but whom I'd never seen as a patient. He was a kind older man who asked me after performing my first ever pelvic exam, "What's that on your finger?"

"A promise ring." It was Tim's gift to me at Christmas a few months earlier.

"Hmm. Well, you might want to call it an engagement ring." He took my hand in both of his and eyed me with caution. "Don't do anything stupid."

Roe vs. Wade was decided in 1973, partly in response to the many back-alley and basement abortions that claimed too many lives prior. I'd heard about wire coat hanger methods and pop-bottle methods to end a pregnancy, but I didn't know how I'd achieve such a thing. No one in my acquaintance had ever done so—at least not that I was aware of. I'd thought little about what might happen next. None of the thoughts that *did* appear included such drastic measures until the doctor brought them to mind. "Don't worry," I said.

It was the height of Việt Nam, anti-war protests,

and feminist sensibility, and Tim and I had just graduated from high school the previous May. We were both itching to be independent. When my pregnancy was confirmed, Tim said, "Let's get married this weekend." I knew this was the right next thing. Because we were minors, our parents would have to sign our marriage license; our next task was to inform them of our plans. Both conversations were as unpleasant as expected, though I can't deny excitement at the prospect of moving into Tim's apartment, which adjoined his parents' home. All agreed to the marriage without shouting or shotgun waving, but there were angry questions and dire predictions for our future.

"I was afraid of this when Tim moved into that apartment." It didn't seem prudent to mention that the apartment hadn't factored into my pregnancy.

"Did you get pregnant on purpose?" I did not. I could count the occasions on which this might have occurred on one hand. It seemed I was hyper-fertile. "How could you let this happen?" and "What will we tell people?" were questions I couldn't answer. Eventually, we agreed to consult our pastor to see if he could perform the ceremony and made plans to visit the courthouse to apply for a marriage license.

The next day, Dad drove me to my 8 a.m. Quantitative Chemistry class as usual and delivered the most painful rebuke so far. His only words: "I'm disappointed in you."

I cried throughout Dr. Smith's lecture.

That same afternoon, Mom came to me in my bedroom and shut the door, a one-time occurrence.

The firm set of her jaw foretold an unhappy conversation. She repeated the question she'd already asked, perhaps expecting a different answer.

"Did you get pregnant on purpose?" It wasn't an accusation, but it wasn't an innocent question.

"Of course not!"

"You know, there are places you can go until the child is born," she suggested, looking away.

"What do you mean?"

She appeared to examine the buttons on her blouse. "No one needs to know you're pregnant. You could go away for a few months and then come back." Her eyes cut back to mine. "Without a baby."

"No!" Despite the unfortunate timing of my pregnancy and my disgraced state, I wanted this child. I'd heard rumors of parents sending their daughters away for the duration of a pregnancy, but Mom's suggestion was not an option. I wouldn't learn until decades later that this had been one sister's fate several years prior. We all thought she'd spent a semester at LSU in Baton Rouge.

Pastor Nelson agreed to marry us with the stipulation that we attend the required premarital session with him. We planned a simple wedding on Saturday, the day before Easter. There were no engraved invitations or festive wedding showers. We didn't order a tiered cake, frothy ginger ale and sherbet punch. We didn't have a streaming rosebud bouquet.Within days, we met for our premarital counseling session, which included a small paperback marriage manual with a section about marital sex. "You can read this section when you have time," he said. I'm not sure which of us was more embarrassed.

The green polyester double-knit, above the knee dress I'd sewn myself for Easter Sunday became my wedding dress. Tim and I walked together up to the church altar, without attendants or a wedding march down the aisle, and said our vows. There was no father handing me over, no tearful mother of the bride. We spent the rest of the Easter weekend at a Holiday Inn in New Orleans, taking advantage of a school holiday on the Monday after Easter. We both resumed classes at McNeese State on Tuesday. I moved my clothes into Tim's apartment and it was done. We were married students and would soon be parents.

The garage apartment Tim had occupied since his senior year of high school was separated from his family's back door by the "pool room," a former carport closed in by my father-in-law to contain the family's pool table. Tim's brother and sister-in-law vacated the apartment just before he moved in. It was compact, but as a first living space, it was better than many, with four tiny rooms. It was heaven to me, representing my much-anticipated independence.

We put together a crib and furnished the rest of the apartment with second-hand furniture, some of it donated by my parents, some left by Tim's brother and sister-in-law. Since the apartment was small, it couldn't hold much. I dropped out of school for the fall semester to prepare for birth. That left me free to pick up additional hours at Lake Charles Memorial Hospital as the lab secretary and to add to our meager savings. Although we'd both worked continuously since high school, our funds evaporated much too quickly. Car insurance for the '65 Ford Falcon Tim's parents gave him for his high school graduation was expensive. We bought a few kitchen essentials and linens to fill in the gaps between a few wedding gifts, a smidgeon of household goods I'd accumulated, and hand-me-downs. Even groceries were sometimes a stretch. His parents' nearness and the rent-free apartment were vital to our survival.

Our son refused to turn right side up—or, more accurately, right side down—for his grand entrance, which presented potential complications at delivery. The possibilities were frightening. Instead, we focused on considering names for our offspring (no family names!) and imagining who he or she would look most like.

The morning my labor started, a week earlier than expected, I'd joined my mother-in-law over her morning coffee to kill time before a scheduled doctor's appointment. I was hoping he wouldn't do another pelvic exam; I already hated them. But I dreaded what was coming, and my mother-in-law, Dottie, was my best support system.

"I'm not sure if I'm in labor," I said, a slight catch in my midsection, "Something feels different."

"Is it painful?"

"Not really. It just feels like a tightness or a cramp. It's different from when the baby moves," I said.

"Is it regular?"

"I don't know. I haven't timed them."

"Well, it's probably not labor," she said, "If it were, you'd know it."

When I got home from my doctor's appointment a few hours later, I reported the results of my pelvic exam, "Dr. McCann said to go to the hospital right away."

Less than an hour later, Dottie helped me check into the Labor Department at Lake Charles Memorial, where I'd worked weekends for a couple of years. My parents came shortly after, and Tim's Aunt Pat also made an appearance as soon as she heard I was in labor. She was as direct as ever. "Phew! Someone's just had an enema!" she declared while fanning the air in the labor suite. In the throes of vise-like uterine contractions and Demerol-induced nausea, I wasn't embarrassed as I might otherwise have been. But this is the statement I most closely associated with Aunt Pat until her death over forty years later.

The doctor turned Marc's head down manually, providing an otherwise uneventful delivery. Physicians these days frown on general anesthesia during labor and delivery because of risks to the infant, but thank God for complete unconsciousness. I didn't know about the reaching in and the turning around until afterward.

When I awoke in the recovery room, shivering and hung over from anesthesia, nurses scurried around me and whispered among themselves. I wondered if I'd given birth to a boy or a girl and if the child was okay, but I was still too groggy to put words together.

"We'll get you to a room soon." One nurse held a cup of water for me to sip from. She said nothing about a child, and I feared her silence had ominous overtones. Maybe my child was stillborn, as Karen's was a few years before. Left alone, I wondered if I'd delivered at all, but running my hands over my abdomen confirmed my womb was empty. When I lifted my arm to brush away a tear running down into my ear, I noticed a second armband on my wrist: Baby Boy Airhart.

We named him Marc Geoffrey. We went home to our tiny apartment, where the long, narrow bedroom accommodated both our double bed and Marc's crib. That Tim's parents were mere steps away was reassuring. They were respectful of our space, but the proximity proved beneficial to all, as my mother-in-law was a loving and generous woman who helped train the naïve young mother of her third grandchild. I'd been so used to life without my mother that I hadn't missed her presence during the labor and delivery, which my parents and Tim's encouraged me through. Not even in my first few weeks as a mother did I consider what my mother might have offered. But I trusted my mother-in-law's care and instructions completely and was deeply grateful for them.

"Hold his head up like this," she said while cradling Marc's head in her right elbow, then sliding his wiggly lower half down into the warm water of her kitchen sink. "Now wet the cloth and wipe his face and chest." She'd motion toward the small washcloth with a nod of her head and direct my cleaning of my son's perfect little body.

"He won't break," she'd say, as we lay Marc on the towel spread out on the counter nearby. Despite my awkwardness and misgivings, she calmly demonstrated and urged me to follow her example.

Within a few weeks, I felt confident enough to enact this routine in our own kitchen sink. I even learned where best to place the washcloth to prevent getting peed on and how to keep water out of Marc's eyes while washing his sparse hair. How he loved his bath! Watching him splash his arms and pump his legs in the water clenched my heart in unexpected ways. I'd prepared clothing, baby furniture, and pediatrician visits, but I'd not prepared my heart for such pleasure in unplanned, ordinary moments. Maybe I *could* be a mother.

Dottie provided other basic lessons in infant care without prodding or heavy-handedness. I welcomed her instruction, but I insisted on practicing the tasks associated with my new role: dressing a body that was never still, sterilizing nipples for the bottles I filled with diluted Similac, rocking a cranky baby in the rocking chair until he gave up the fight and slept. I learned to read his moods and predict his needs—imperfectly, but adequately—and respond in ways that would keep our son alive and his mother sane.

Soon after Marc's birth, Tim enrolled in an electronics program at the local vocational-technical school, and I took a full-time position at the hospital. Hellbent on complete independence, and counter to all reason, we moved into our own apartment across town. What we could afford was in a questionable neighborhood, but we bought a few cheap furnishings and occupied our own space for the first time.

While the apartment was functional and clean, it wasn't air-conditioned. Without air-conditioning, the hot and humid south Louisiana summer months were almost unbearable, especially with an infant. The greatest consolation was a huge vent fan installed just below the one living room window. When we flipped the switch, it felt as though it might suck the hair right off our heads and sounded like a turbojet on takeoff. On the upside, the breeze it created and the background noise could lull the baby to sleep.

When, less than a year after our move into the apartment, Tim's parents offered one of their several rental houses for our use if we made the needed repairs, we rejoiced at the prospect of homeownership. As every seasoned homeowner knows, we'd never need another hobby.

The house on Ninth Avenue was in frightful condition, but it was ours and represented greater stability. When we first surveyed the house in 1972, not only was the carport piled floor to ceiling with trash, but the bathtub was filled with garbage, kitchen waste and desiccated roach corpses included. Cracked or half-missing linoleum floor tiles covered the floors of every room, kitchen cabinet doors hung awkwardly from their hinges, and uniform gashes in the sheetrock pockmarked the living room walls. Someone had evidently practiced their axe-throwing skills on them. After stiffing my father-in-law, Allen, for a couple months' rent, his tenants had slipped away one night without warning. Allen agreed to deed the house to us if we'd make it habitable and take on the small mortgage that remained. His offer was a godsend.

With help from friends and family members, we patched and painted walls and cabinets, laid down cheap carpeting all over the house, and cleaned out the garbage through the hot months of early summer. Tim built a makeshift bar in the kitchen to expand counter space, and I accessorized cabinet doors with brightly flowered stick-on rolled vinyl, a la "mod" decorating trends. Transforming the three-bedroom, one-bath wood-frame house into a livable—even cheerful—home was sweaty, backbreaking work but well worth it. We moved in a couple of days before President Nixon resigned that August and left the White House, about a month before our son's first birthday. I watched the black and white TV coverage of Nixon boarding Air Force One while I unpacked our clothes and hung them in the tiny bedroom closet.

The house was convenient to our jobs, and I soon located a place for Marc in child care at the New Nursery a few blocks away so I could return to full-time work. The proprietor, Kitty King, was to become a caring and encouraging presence in our lives for the next seven years.

Marc fell in love with her. "See Kitty King?" he'd ask at breakfast.

"Yes," I'd say most days, and he would respond with a grin while stuffing cereal into his mouth and nodding in satisfaction. He'd repeat to himself, in a statement this time, "See Kitty King."

On my days off, I'd say, "Not today." He'd

sometimes cry and ask for her again. I was happy he loved her so much, but did he cry for me when he was with her? I didn't want to know the answer.

The feminist movement of the late 60s and early 70s—sometimes called the second wave movement—demanded equal rights for women in many arenas and provided bookends to the antiwar protests and free love movements. It was a period of great cultural change, but our focus on staying out of debt and learning how to parent blurred our consciousness and left little time or energy for events outside our immediate world. To this day, I can't name or identify much early 70s music or artists; by the late 70s, the music was so ridiculous, I didn't *want* to identify any of it. My contributions to the feminist movement were minimal: I insisted on working full time (actually, this was a necessity), I went braless when I could, and I sent our son to child care—with a *bottle*. Meanwhile, we were clawing our way up to solvency.

A couple of years after moving to the Ninth Avenue home, we leveraged its sale to purchase a slightly larger home in the nearby suburb of Sulphur, Louisiana. I returned to college when Marc was a preschooler and worked most weekends and weekday evenings when I could get a shift. Tim had cashed in on his electronics license by taking a technical position at a rural telephone company close to our new home. We settled into a relatively comfortable life in the new neighborhood, making a few friends and growing more confident in our ability to thrive as a family.

Tim built Marc a treehouse in one of the towering trees in our large backyard, which he once fell from and broke his wrist. Marc and the other boys near his age who lived on our street climbed in and out of the tree, explored the wooded area behind our block of houses, and then tracked mud and slime onto our floors with typical boyish enthusiasm. We relished this period of relative emotional and financial stability.

After moving to Sulphur, we decided we were ready to have another child. This time, we would choose the timing. I discontinued birth control pills, and consistent with the earlier evidence of our ability to conceive, I became pregnant almost at once. Laboratory tests for pregnancy in the 70s required a second missed period for confirmation. Unlike today, when it seems a woman can get up from the bed after having sex, pee on a plastic test strip, and watch for the plus sign, the tube test for HCG (the hormone produced by the cells of a placenta and excreted into urine) just wasn't that sensitive. It didn't keep me from trying, though. Since one of my job functions in the lab was performing the HCG tests, I added my sample to a test run every few days with great anticipation. It only took a couple of weeks to confirm what I already suspected.

I'd recognized the signs much earlier: the breast soreness, the full bladder (no matter how often I emptied it) and occasional nausea. It was clear my body remembered what to do. By the time the tube test was positive, we were testing the sounds of possible names and had begun planning nursery décor. My abdomen, somewhat slack from the earlier pregnancy, pooched at once as if it recognized its role in announcing my status.

The news delighted our families. Tim's younger sister, frustrated with three nephews but no nieces, warned, "If it's another boy, just leave him at the hospital." I hoped not to disappoint her. In fact, the hope of having a daughter was so great that I almost couldn't make myself consider boys' names. I loved Marc more fiercely than I'd ever imagined possible. But a *daughter*. Still yearning for the mother-daughter bond I'd missed, my hopes went into overdrive; I wanted a fresh start, a do-over. Maybe I'd do better the second time around. I'd be the mother and not the daughter, but it was a kind of connection I'd never had, idealized to mythic proportions. Already my expectations struck against me.

We'd been planning a Florida vacation that summer, and we didn't see any reason to let a new pregnancy interfere with our plans. I felt fine. Marc was not yet four years old and enthralled with the Goofy and Mickey characters he'd seen in the Disney story books that were delivered to our home each month from the Disney Book Club. We drove from Louisiana to Orlando on the first day and pitched a tent at Jellystone Park campground. Saving money on our sleeping arrangements was the only way we could afford Disney World at all.

On the afternoon of our first day at the park, I noticed a few small spots of blood in my underwear after a bathroom visit. I ignored them. A few hours later, I felt the tightness of cramps in my midsection.

There were more spots, but I didn't want to ruin anyone's fun.

By evening, it was clear the spotting and cramps were increasing. When I told Tim about it, he encouraged me to call my obstetrician back home.

"Go to a hotel," my doctor said, "Take down your tent and move to a hotel with air conditioning and an actual bed. Don't get out of bed unless you have to." My doctor wasn't given to ordering patients around, and his instructions frightened me. It felt like an accusation.

When I passed a clod of bloody fetal tissue into the toilet that evening, I called my doctor's emergency number, and he advised me to go to the emergency room. At the hospital in Kissimmee, just outside Orlando, I was admitted overnight for a morning D&C (dilation and curettage) procedure, which consisted of having my uterus scraped clean of any lingering fetal tissue to avoid infection or other complications of miscarriage.

When the doctor came to check on me the next morning, I was tearful. I feared something I'd done—like tent camping in the heat of July—had somehow killed that cloudy red clump of cells growing inside me.

"Why did this happen?" I said weakly, twisting the thin sheet in my hands.

My cramps had disappeared in the surgical suite as surely as my hope. What was wrong with this body, I wondered, that it couldn't do what it was designed to do and nourish the child we'd chosen to create?

The doctor shrugged, "Sometimes there's something wrong with the baby, and it just doesn't take." After examining me, he advised me not to have sex for four weeks, to give my body a rest. "Don't worry," he said. "You couldn't have prevented this." I was pronounced fit and discharged.

We spent one more evening in the darkened hotel room—me in the bed, sporadically crying, and Tim distracting Marc in the hotel's playground—before we drove back to Lake Charles and our ordinary routines. I felt I'd left an important part of me in Florida and couldn't shake the feeling that I could've prevented the miscarriage, that I'd taken too much for granted. I said little during the twelve-hour drive, in between sniffling and dabbing my eyes with a tissue and blowing my nose.

"What's wrong with Mommy?" Marc said. He'd been subdued the previous few days, despite his curtailed Disney adventure. I wanted to pull him across the seat and into my lap to comfort us both.

"I'll be all right." My puffy eyes and wet cheeks contradicted the smile I sent over my shoulder. "Mommy was sick for a while, but I'm getting better." We hadn't told him about either the pregnancy or the miscarriage; we were just getting used to the emotional turmoil ourselves. Tim had called our families to tell them what was happening, and one family member remarked that maybe we shouldn't have gone camping after all. It was like a punch to my aching gut.

Outside Orlando, a billboard appeared ahead on the interstate advertising a gift shop with the picture of a little girl, sad that no one had thought to bring her a souvenir. In large, bold letters, the sign asked,

"Are you forgetting someone?" Tim and I looked at each other, and I muffled sobs with a tissue. It would be months before I could forget who we'd left behind.

Per my doctor's instructions, we waited four weeks as he advised, and again we proved our fertility. We were more cautious this time in announcing my condition and making plans, but it became clear my "rebound" pregnancy would take. We focused our hope on a healthy child and normal delivery.

My sister Sue and I'd first become pregnant about the same time, and if it hadn't been for my miscarriage, we would have delivered within days of each other. Her daughter Niki was born in December that year, and while I was happy she'd broken the streak of grandsons in my family, I cried in disappointment. In my hormonally charged, superstitiously oriented state, I thought that only one of us could have the girl we both wanted; she already had a son too. I was certain this was a sign I'd have a boy and worked hard over the last few months of my pregnancy at coming to terms with the prospect of another son. There's nothing worse than being surprised by disappointment; I'd much rather be surprised by what I'm afraid to hope for. This time, my hopes materialized.

Kelly Denise was born healthy the following March after an uncomplicated delivery. I would have my second chance to become the mother I expected myself to be. My heart raced with anticipation at the sight of tiny pink and green dresses, as I folded them warm from the dryer and stacked them into neat piles. I'd painted the dresser and rocking chair white and sewed colorful cotton curtains for her bedroom window, the epitome of perfection. I still had a lot to learn about that particular myth.

At Kelly's first visit to the pediatrician, he suggested that her bowed legs needed correction to avoid problems with her gait when she began to walk. He recommended a footboard device with special shoes screwed into place, something like a modern snowboard with bindings. We slipped her feet into the shoes, which we turned gradually outward. She hated her feet being restricted and cried when we put it on her each night before bed. It made us feel a bit cruel, but we persisted for a few months until her doctor pronounced her legs straight enough.

I didn't realize until I read in Mother's hospital admission notes that my legs had also bowed at birth. According to mother's chart, "the patient was distressed when her obstetrician recommended that the baby should be examined by a pediatrician." She was in the throes of paranoia by then, only a few months before her commitment. The contour of my legs was only one of several factors which pushed her over the brink of madness at an already emotionally charged time. In contrast, I experienced ordinary postpartum anxiety that resolved itself within weeks. I can relate to her apprehension, however. In the years since my birth, correction for bowed legs is only attempted if they don't straighten on their own within a few years, as they normally do. Neither my mother nor I should have been made to worry at all.

If Marc's infant demands exhausted me, Kelly's 3:00 a.m. episodes of colic painfully tested my endurance. Her projectile vomiting was so explosive it sometimes splattered the wall behind us when I propped her over my shoulder for burping. Her doctor recommended predigested formula, which smelled going in the bottle almost worse than what hit the wall later.

During her third year, she experienced what I later learned were night terrors, jolting the entire family out of our deepest sleep in the early morning hours several times a week. I'd never heard of such things and assumed she was having nightmares. Tim and I tried everything we could think of to calm her, but nothing seemed to work. When I tried to hold her on my lap to soothe her, she fought and scratched—while screaming at maximum volume—as though I were trying to smother her. Afterward, she'd wet her bed, meaning a late-night bed change. If I brought her to the bathroom to use the toilet during an episode, she'd pull away from me, then pee on the floor in her nightclothes, all the while shrieking and kicking, sometimes injuring herself. Some nights, she screeched so loudly and for so long I was afraid our neighbors would call protective services. The incidents resolved by the time she was four, but they left me exhausted and wary, wondering what I might have done to cause them.

Still, my conviction persisted that mothering a daughter would provide something I'd lost by not being mothered, which multiplied the stakes. I engaged in *intentional* mothering in ways I hadn't had the luxury of earlier when it was more critical to be intentional about staggering which bills we could pay in what order. Our children had different temperaments, and I found that caring for one toddler hadn't prepared me to care for the second. I hesitated to ask for advice from Mom or Dottie, as it would call attention to a weakness I was afraid to admit. The mother I might have sought advice from was long gone, had never been available at all. Perhaps if Mother had remained whole, I would have asked, "Am I doing any of this right?" Or more practical questions like "How do I teach my kids to care about other people?" My relationship with Ruby wasn't close enough for such questions, and I feared imposing on Dottie's kindness too much. Maybe I was just stubborn. The questions remained unasked and unanswered. It became clear I'd never live up to my own standards, and how could I when I attributed God-like qualities to a mother? In addition, I didn't recognize the limitations posed by my personality.

I was sometimes too shy to insist on having my own needs met and also failed to advocate strongly enough for my children's needs if it meant confronting others. I'm still haunted by the look on Kelly's face when I let a friend of hers walk out of the house with her special set of fruit-scented markers in her backpack. We all knew they were there. I didn't know what to say with the friend's mother on the doorstep.

After the door closed, I said, "We'll buy you another set of markers." But I'd already shown myself to be a coward.

There were arguments or disagreements with both of our children that led to sulks and angry outbursts, some of them mine. Those contentious moments were punctuated by heart-bursting incidents of unexpected joy, however. No one had warned me about these either: the way my heart would swell when our son announced his selection as first chair trombone in the fifth-grade band or when our daughter read her first chapter book on her own. I hadn't anticipated mirroring both my children's joys and sorrows or the visceral connections that persisted years after giving birth. Motherhood had indeed captured my heart and soul—just not in the ways I expected.

Southeast Louisiana Hospital
Henke, Barbara
Hospital Number 201

Selected Psychiatric Notes

February 12, 1957:

Barbara asked attendants to take her to seclusion because she was mad at the whole world.

February 24, 1957:

Barbara went into the bathroom and spit her med out in the toilet and flushed.

March 11, 1957:

Patient had a very bad seizure at 5:10 AM. Body was stiff and jerking. Foaming at the mouth. Seizure lasted 10 minutes. Nurse notified.

March 18, 1957:

Hanna M. told Elaine that Barbara had thrown a cig at her. Elaine grabbed Barbara by the collar and slapped her, pulled her hair, and kicked her. Barbara did the same to Elaine. Elaine pulled two hands full of hair out of Barbara's head. Barbara screamed and hollered.

Seemed wild. Transferred to C-1. No injury that we could see.

XVII

Motherhood 102

"I love you to pieces," my mother-in-law would say as she wrapped her arms around my children in a tight squeeze and rocked them side-to-side. They'd giggle and hug her back, then run off to play their games, secure in knowing they were loved. It was a simple thing, but it sometimes brought tears to my eyes.

I was eighteen before anyone told me they loved me, and I did the most sensible thing I could do and married him. The words didn't come as easily to him as they did to his mother, but at eighteen he was more capable of them than I was.

"Mom used to tell us kids she loved us to pieces all the time," Tim said once of himself and his five siblings. "There was nothing better than her big bear hugs."

My father never said, "I love you." His actions proved loving, but I'm not sure I fully understood the emotion until I was nearly grown. The words could still be awkward in my mouth, but my mother-in-law taught me it's a mother's job to say them.

Dorothy "Dottie" Airhart was the most unselfish mother I knew. With few exceptions, she would happily offer a ride, babysit, or share a meal, or just a cup of coffee and a slice of pie with my husband and me. Since we lived a few yards from their back door during the first year of our marriage, our comings and goings overlapped. Dottie gave subtle advice and made clear through expression and action what she felt were the best mothering techniques. "They've got to eat a peck of dirt before they're grown," was the response to a pacifier dropped on the floor or to my obsessive bottle and rubber nipple-boiling. Immunologists agree with her theory: it is healthy for a child to be exposed to the microorganisms that surround us.

During afternoon rest times, stretched out in front of afternoon soap operas on TV, she declared that her strategy for most things was "the path of least resistance." We laughed over that, but I knew that hour each afternoon was a much-needed period of rest, and I interrupted it. I felt accepted and relaxed in their home in a way I hadn't when living with my merged family, where I still felt awkward and misplaced. After her unofficial rest time, Dottie prepared coffee and treats—cookies, pies, or cake, fresh from the oven—for assorted kin, including my father-in-law and her brother, who walked up to the house from the workshop where they produced duck and game calls for national sporting goods chains and department stores. This tradition persisted for years until a stroke forced her to the sidelines.

Dottie's look of disapproval—a rare occurrence—taught me to temper my frustration when calming a fussy baby or toddler. One day when Marc was an infant, and we'd joined Dottie for her soap opera rest, he fretted over some discomfort that wasn't obvious. He didn't respond to my first efforts to calm him and continued to cry. When I tried rocking him over my shoulder more vigorously than necessary, he cried harder. Exasperated, I dropped him on the sofa beside me and crossed my arms in defeat. Marc continued to wail. Dottie said nothing. With brows furrowed and head tilted, her eyes held mine for a few seconds. Without a word, she reached over to pick up my son, laid him lengthwise along her legs, and rocked him side to side. "What's the matter, little boy?" she crooned, "What do you need?" Marc sputtered and stared up into his grandmother's eyes, sucking in the breath he'd been holding.

I wanted to slink out the door. No condemnation could have better shown where I'd failed and where her gentle response had succeeded. Once Marc quieted, Dottie placed him back in my arms with an encouraging smile. In the space of a few minutes, she'd made clear both her assessment of my impatience and her confidence I could do better. I was determined to validate her trust, and my aptitude grew, but it grew slowly. Our children were sometimes guilty of deliberate misbehavior and accidental mishaps, as all children are, and they still provoked knee-jerk responses.

Once, when Kelly was a toddler and running through the house, giggling with joy in a game of chase, her foot caught on an electric cord and she pulled down a living room lamp, which shattered on the floor. We had few items of value, with hand-me-down or cheap furnishings. The *lamp*, though. I'd loved it when I saw it in a local department store, not the Kmart I customarily shopped at, and spent more on it than was logical. For me, it symbolized the choice of an object I loved, not merely a necessary item chosen because it was affordable.

"Kelly!" I screamed from too many feet away while it tottered and fell as though in slow motion.

Kelly froze, then turned toward me with wide eyes and an open mouth. Tears had already formed.

"No! Stop running!" I yanked one of her arms and swatted her rump with an open palm. It hurt her feelings more than her backside, but it was just as damaging. My body shook with irritation.

Kelly sobbed in between gasps while I picked up the pieces of the lamp and fumed at her. I was suddenly struck by the picture of my mother screaming and hitting in the driveway of our home when I was six and hid behind my sister, Karen. It was the scream of a crazy woman, and I'd just copied her. I pulled Kelly to me and fell back on the sofa, holding my daughter's shuddering body until we both stopped shaking.

I was disgusted with myself; that was not the mother I wanted to be.

"Bye, Mom," Kelly walked through her kindergarten classroom door without a backward glance in 1981. I hesitated for a few breaths as other mothers hugged their children and streamed around me, excited to begin this new adventure. I hadn't realized how hard it would be to let her walk away from me. We'd visited the classroom during "Meet the Teacher" night and thought her teacher seemed a kind soul, but it felt as though I were sending this small young girl, my youngest child, into an unfamiliar land.

The year Kelly started kindergarten, we'd just moved to Jenks, Oklahoma, outside Tulsa, when Tim took a job with a telecommunications company called United Video. It was a great opportunity for both Tim's career and our family. Through the summer after our move, I'd been home with Marc and Kelly, appreciating the time to get acquainted with our new community: climbing on the antique rail car and "monkey bars" at the Jenks America Park, listening in on children's story hours at the library, and stocking up on school clothes and supplies at Woodland Hills Mall. With Kelly in school, the cat and I would be alone in our quiet house all morning.

I recognized Kelly's abrupt goodbye as nervousness rather than actual dismissal. And that's why I hesitated, biting back the question my heart was screaming, "Don't you need me?" My independent, determined daughter had decided not to cling, so I turned and walked down the hall.

I cried all the way home.

Our children transitioned to a new school or a new city with surprising confidence—and there were many during their childhoods. Invariably, when Tim's employers recognized his value to their company, he was offered job transfers or promotions. These changes took us from Lake Charles, Louisiana,to Port Arthur, Texas; to Tulsa, Oklahoma; to Dallas, Texas; to suburban Duncanville, Texas; then back to Tulsa, Oklahoma. We sometimes leased for a year before buying a home, which meant a transfer to another school district. Marc lived in ten different homes and had attended seven different districts by the time he graduated. At each new phase, I worried. Had we done enough to prepare them? Had I been a good enough mother? Second-guessing can become a disease.

When Marc started kindergarten four years before his sister, I'd been relieved to have only one child left at home—it meant fewer disputes to settle—and he enjoyed his role as big brother and trailblazer. He reveled in telling us the stories of his day, and I enjoyed hearing them.

"Hey Mom!" he said once on the way home from Tyrrell Elementary, just a few blocks from our home in Port Arthur. "Did you know some cookies float on top of water but some sink?"

"No. Really?"

"Yeah. Chocolate chip sinks. Well, some of them did." He explained it depended on how many chocolate chips were in the cookies.

"I guess that means the best cookies sink," I said.

"I don't know. I like vanilla wafers, too, and they floated."

Like his mother, Marc was fascinated with science and the natural world, and a good student overall. Almost daily, he launched into descriptions of lab experiments, lessons and group activities, or books they'd read. Kelly was similarly passionate about learning. Their enthusiasm was infectious. Hearing them describe their school experiences was the best part of every day.

My good friend Erv Janssen, a child psychiatrist, often speaks about the amazing resilience of children who experience "good enough parenting." Each time I hear him, I think, *Thank God!*

As our children demonstrated their differences in temperament, I often changed tactics, but I felt like I was juggling Jell-O. We'd moved to Port Arthur, Texas, after my husband's first job transfer in 1978 when our kids were six and two. I was eager to assert my independence as a daughter and stepdaughter in a family that exhausted me with expectations, mine *and* theirs, at the same time my own children were becoming individuals.

The questions I might have asked a mother went unspoken. Instead, I depended on observational skills to sense what I needed. I was more likely to take parenting cues from Angela and Tisha's mom two doors down than ask family members for advice about navigating disagreements with teachers or worries about healthy behaviors. Marc and Kelly both made friends in our new neighborhood, and I looked for excuses to knock on their doors to retrieve my children or to borrow an egg or stick of butter. I'm not sure that would have been different if my mother had survived. I know many daughters who shy away from asking their mothers questions. This calls Jane Flax's research to mind about what can be dicey relationships between mothers and daughters, even daughters who've spent their entire lives close to their mothers.

"Marc is so polite," Marc's friend Sean's mother remarked once when I arrived at their door to bring him home for dinner, "He's always courteous and considerate."

Who? I wanted to ask. My son, Marc? The same son who tried to light a fire—"just a little one, Mom"—in the backyard with the book of matches he'd swiped from his father's collection? The child who left mud streaks from his tennies all the way down the hall and sweat-soaked shirt and pants in a wad on his bedroom floor?

"Thank you," I said, "We enjoy having Sean at our house, too."

A peek inside someone else's home life and seeing my children through someone else's eyes could be instructive ... and reassuring. When Angela and Tisha's dad (a fundamentalist preacher) was caught, literally, with his pants down, the parents split. This development shocked me, but led to the suspicion that our family wasn't as precarious as I feared. I had to look elsewhere for parenting models. Dr. T. Berry Brazelton, who wrote a column in each issue of *Parent's Magazine* (which I devoured like a starving woman in the presence of cherry cheesecake) was a safe bet. I soaked up every morsel of wisdom.

I didn't dare ask Mom for advice, remembering her predictions about my failure at marriage and parenthood, her suggestion that I give away my child. Requesting guidance from either her or Dottie seemed an admission of failure, and I refused to admit I didn't know what the hell I was doing. A mother's reassurance would've been welcome, but since I'd gotten by so far without it, I couldn't have identified what that might look like.

My invented version of a mother was as idealistic as it was wrongheaded. I'd wanted a mother who loved without regard to her own needs, but such a mother doesn't exist. Understanding dawned bit by bit. Instead, I needed a much wiser mother, someone with experience in taming temper tantrums, correcting rude or hurtful behavior with loving, calm remarks, and managing disappointments, no matter the circumstance. That mother didn't exist either, and during my deepest, darkest, sleepless nights of worry, when I needed a mother the most, it felt I had no one to turn to.

Still, I was becoming more confident. Colleagues and friends shared their parenting nightmares, which taught me to more readily trust my instincts. Meltdowns at the grocery checkout could be dealt with by substituting a Little Golden Book for the candy bar my children screamed for; I preferred engaging their minds to their stomachs. Sometimes consequences of their actions, missteps in friendships or dating attempts, were better teachers than I could be, and I let my kids learn from the mistakes. There were also lessons I neglected to teach, like how to apologize for causing painful offense or how to have hard conversations with people you love, because I hadn't learned them myself.

In 1982, when the children were six and almost eleven, I turned back to developing the professional persona I'd paused before our move to Oklahoma. I'd tried being a full-time mom for a couple of years before Kelly started kindergarten, but I didn't have the skills or the patience for it. Now that she was in first grade, I turned back to a professional career. We moved from our rental in Jenks and purchased a home in the north Tulsa suburb of Owasso that summer. I found a medical technology job at the American Red Cross Blood Center in Tulsa and scrambled for suitable child care, the scourge of working mothers everywhere.

At least in the lab, I felt useful and capable. There were no skinned elbows and knees to dab with peroxide while uttering soothing comments over the wails and insistences that, "Ow, that hurts!" I was no longer frustrated by refusals to take afternoon naps. Not mine—I'd never have refused a nap. There was no more barging into my bedroom while demanding, "keep (insert child's name here) out of my room!" For hours each day, there was a respite from "she's/he's *looking* at me!"

There were workplace dramas and jealousies,

some just as childish as the ones taking place at home, but I could leave those dramas in the lab, while the dramas at home were more sustained. At the end of a day, certifying the safe release of blood products to hospital patients was rewarding; it was a responsibility I was proud to contribute to. It appealed to my sense of worth, as well as my need for structure and organization. Blood was one of four types; it was simply positive or negative for hepatitis or HIV, and our procedures defined steps for each possibility.

When Kelly's school called during her first-grade year and asked me to come pick her up, after she complained of a stomachache, it took me an hour to reach a point in the lab assays I was performing to leave work. "Another student went home from her class today with stomachache," the nurse said, hinting at copycat symptoms.

Kelly perked up as soon as she buckled up her seatbelt. "You *do* care about me," she said. Her smug grin said it all, her healing immediate.

"Of course I do. Did you think I wouldn't come? I would've been here sooner, but I had to finish testing before I could leave." She just shrugged, satisfied. It was the first full-time job I'd held in her memory, and she wasn't sure until she saw me that I'd choose to come for her, the stomachache only anxiety. At least I wouldn't have to clean up vomit in the car.

Returning to the workforce was a salve for me—I felt at home in the laboratory; I knew I was good at what I did. Confidence grew despite lingering anxiety about my mental health prospects and both propelled me toward breaking the code of silence I'd honored for over twenty years. Breaking it felt like betrayal, however.

Graceland is one of the oldest cemeteries in Lake Charles and includes graves dating back to the Civil War. Next to it is Orange Grove Cemetery, and across the street is an even older, unnamed area of graves inside a chain-link fence. Because of a high water table in Louisiana, many of the graves are in mausoleums or aboveground crypts.

The question I posed caught Dad off guard. I'm not sure what he expected, but his look of confusion is what I'll remember best about this visit to Graceland Cemetery in 1982.

"What was my mother like?" I tried to keep my voice from quaking after we'd found her headstone amid the maze of marble, cement, and stone and after tedious winding up and down rows. "You never talked about her. What was she like?" This was the hardest question I'd ever had to ask.

"I thought you weren't interested," Dad said, head tilted and brows pinched, "You never asked."

"No," I sputtered, tears threatening, "I didn't think I could."

After decades of silence about my mother, it seemed improper—even dangerous—to ask. In part, I feared betraying an implicit family pact of silence. Maybe I feared what I might learn. I was still ashamed of my proximity to mental illness and my continued longing for a mother.

Good lord! You're a mother, already. Put on your big girl panties and move on! That self-talk worked ... until it didn't. My children's mental health might depend on my own, and I wasn't yet sure I could count on stability. Before I asked Dad to take me to the cemetery, when I resolved to shatter the silence, I began at the wrong place.

I first consulted a pastor who also practiced hypnotism as part of his professional counseling services, and I hoped hypnosis would help to uncover submerged memories. This seemed the safest avenue I could pursue. No one else needed to know what I might learn.

I'm not sure if I'm not a fit candidate for hypnosis or whether the pastor wasn't a fit candidate for practicing it. Despite complying with his prompts—Raise the fingers on your right hand. Now raise your right hand, and so on—I'm pretty sure I didn't enter a state of hypnosis. I didn't feel my arms grow light and lifting. I didn't slip off into a state of semiconsciousness, and I learned nothing.

The pastor prompted me to ask Dad my questions, though. His suggestion proved his greatest contribution to my quest. Voicing questions was what I'd dreaded doing all along, but I had to admit the nonhypnotizing pastor was right. A few months later, I followed through. Tim encouraged a trip to Lake Charles to talk with my father. I began by asking Dad over the telephone if he would take me to Graceland to find my mother's grave. It was an excuse to see him one-on-one, a rarity, and to ask him the questions I'd pondered for years.

At twenty-nine, I was about the same age my parents had been when my mother was first diagnosed with schizophrenia and when they had three young children. I needed to know I wasn't subject to developing or passing on her condition. I was amazed that Dad was surprised by my question. How could he not understand how vital it was to know who my mother had been?

I hadn't been to Graceland since the day we buried her sixteen years before, and I wanted to see her grave with adult eyes. I'd also wanted my father to myself for this conversation, so Tim offered to bring the kids to visit with Mom while Dad and I went to the cemetery.

"What was she like?" was all I could manage before the trembling and tearing up started. Twenty-nine years of confusing and ironclad emotional control threatened to explode, most of them regulated by the one inviolable law governing outward expressions throughout my childhood: *Don't talk about it; it's not normal. We're not normal.* Because this law hadn't ever been articulated, it was deeply codified. Silence often has much deeper consequences than speech.

I'll never know if Dad felt pain or relief when he talked about Mother and their life together. They only had six or seven good years before schizophrenia ushered in thirteen years of hell for them both: he struggling with the demands of caring from a distance for a sick wife and three young children at home, and she feeling confused, angry, and deserted by turns—not to mention tormented by her disease.

Dad had been contentedly remarried for fifteen years in 1982. It's possible recalling my mother was more difficult because of ordinary memory lapses than the pain of recall, though. He didn't realize that while he was striving to forget the awful details, I was desperate to remember… *anything*.

"Bobbie loved to play bridge and Ping-Pong; she loved reading, poetry and wonderful music," He recited a bullet-point list of Bobbie's likes and dislikes, and I suppose they're better than nothing. She was an excellent typist and enjoyed sewing. She loved daiquiris. Blue was her favorite color. "But she told me blue was *not* my color." He'd always refused to wear blue clothing, but I never understood why. Mom knew it; the entire family did. We disagreed with it, but he was steadfast in this until his death. Bizarre as it seems, this may have been the most concrete expression of Mother's legacy in his life. She'd shaped all our lives in subtle ways.

"Not long after your brother was born, things weren't as they should've been," Dad told me as we stood between headstones in the cemetery, "It was a while before I could see patterns in her behavior, and when she was pregnant with you, things got a lot worse." Her insistence that her obstetrician was in love with her was too dramatic to ignore.

"I've never felt so helpless," Dad said with a sigh, "Your mother's rounds of violence or ridiculous fantasies were frightening." When he became convinced she might harm my sister, brother, and me, he saw no other option but to have her committed judicially, at the recommendation of her psychiatrist. She wouldn't agree to hospitalization voluntarily.

"It was the only time I'd cried as an adult," he said.

"I hired housekeepers to help, and when she was home for visits, she complained they were bossing her around. But I couldn't trust her to take care of you." Mrs. Bourgeois was the first woman Dad hired. "But she died after a couple of years," Dad said, "You were still pretty young. Even after she died, her husband took you kids fishing sometimes." After Mrs. Bourgeois, there was a Mrs. Leger, who I remember vaguely and whose red hair fascinated me. After her came Mrs. Brown, who I remember well, and who was influential in my early years. Suzy was the last young woman who looked after us for a few hours after school, and I liked her a lot, but she only stayed until Karen could supervise us.

Mother's doctors tried treatments, the best available, but she got worse. "When she was well, though, your mother was a beautiful and loving person." Maybe that was all I needed to know.

After our conversation at Graceland, we rejoined the family and Mom brought out a box of memorabilia she wanted me to have. "Here's your mother's photo album." She handed me the black leather album bound with silk cord. "And her hat box. Isn't it fancy?" Mom was glad to regain the space in their closet, but the generosity of these gifts overwhelmed me. "It's got your mother's married initials stamped on it," Mom said of the hatbox, "See?" I'd owned almost nothing that belonged to my mother. Without these artifacts, my mother's existence had seemed an illusion.

My father and I never discussed my mother again; he never mentioned her name in the following twelve years or before his sudden death in 1994. He'd long since, and I think gratefully, forgotten about that difficult period of his life.

More than ten years after he died, when I received my mother's hospital file from Southeast Louisiana State Hospital in 2005, I learned my father's side of the story in his own words, and while the pain was raw. In the meantime, I had his memories of events. This knowledge was sufficient for a time, as I passed what I considered the "dangerous" years when I might also contract schizophrenia, and my job and family responsibilities consumed me.

The last years of parenting were a blur, busy with the kids' activities and our own. I had little time to reflect or dwell on insecurities amid piano lessons, band practice, church youth group, Boy Scouts, and assorted crises. That busyness contributed to frayed tensions and disappointments, which I was sometimes unable to manage well.

Marc graduated from high school in 1989, after another of Tim's promotions and a few days before we moved to Tulsa a second time. Marc stayed put at North Texas University, just north of the Dallas suburb we'd lived in throughout his high school years. While I'd been eager to send him off to kindergarten, my response to his college leave-taking was tearful. Tim and I both worried that whatever we should've taught him or however we'd prepared him for adulthood hadn't been enough. For the first few weeks, Marc called with news or problems we couldn't remedy from Oklahoma. He didn't know how to find meals when his class ended after his dorm cafeteria closed. His math textbook was out of stock in the bookstore. Before long, he learned how to access resources on campus and threw himself into college life, where we assumed he was happy and busy with school and social activities. We sometimes had to track him down just to satisfy ourselves that he was still alive.

Meanwhile, Kelly finished high school in Tulsa, struggling to balance an obsession with academic success and a need to express herself through music and other creative pursuits to prove her worth. Working part-time, I was more available to be supportive, but she turned toward peers to satisfy her relationship needs. The presumed insult of a classmate could crush her, and my attempts to comfort or advise her crushed her again, which perplexed me. I'm again haunted by the conflict mothers and daughters can arouse in each other, according to social scientists like Flax. While it may be ordinary or inevitable, much of the blame lies at the feet of the mother, who should presumably "know better" as the adult. It's clear I did *not* know better.

During this same period, Tim and I both completed graduate programs that sapped our time, our energy, and our patience, as our daughter's need for independence grew. Strife that took an emotional toll on her—and on me—marked those years. Ill-equipped to alleviate her struggles, I too easily dismissed her pain, which exacerbated it for us both, and which I am still trying to reconcile.

I questioned the ideal image of a mother with godlike qualities that I pressured myself to be, yet I felt helpless to give up on trying to hit the invented target. A lingering sense of unfinished business troubled me when Kelly left home for Texas Tech University in 1994, where she seemed to flourish as her brother had done at North Texas. Her departure meant the end of our active parenting career. Whether we felt we'd completed our jobs or not, whether we'd been good enough parents, our children were launched. No do-overs.

Despite all the missed or misused opportunities, we did some things right—you'd almost have to wish for failure not to stumble on an occasional success. Consistent bedtimes and reading routines created structure and a lifelong desire for learning; religious education instilled a value of compassion for others. We supported them during challenging times, even when their difficulties were of their own making.

Our children's responses taught me much of what I needed to know about parenting and about relationships. When they were young, I often tried to fulfill what I perceived as our children's *wants*, drawing on memories of my childhood wants, but that was misguided. The greatest lesson I learned from parenting is this: what a child wants is not always what a child needs. My children grew up and became parents themselves (and *excellent* ones) before I recognized the difference. I'd spent too long grieving a lost relationship with a mother who couldn't fulfill my wants and had instead been nurtured by a life that provided what I *needed*. The puzzle pieces didn't look at all as I'd expected, but they filled the puzzle in more or less rewarding ways.

Southeast Louisiana Hospital
Henke, Barbara
Hospital Number 201

Selected Psychiatric Notes

March 31, 1957:

Patient was up smoking and talking with attendants and patient Florence K. About 5:00 AM they started singing and dancing in the large dayroom. Attendant had to ask them to please be quieter as there were two patients sleeping in the dayroom. Patient seems very worried that her husband may not take her back.

May 11, 1957:

10:25 AM Barbara came up to nurse's station door and asked about Pineville Hospital. Said she heard it was a hospital for adults with retarded minds. Attendant C. told her to ask the doctor about Pineville hospital. Barbara asked Mr. T. about her brain operation she had and said she could not remember when she had the operation. Patient said she has six stitches a quarter of an inch long on the side of her head.

XVIII
The End of the Quest

If I'd ever attempted to envision the extended family I was born into, I couldn't have imagined a more disparate reality. When I finally met my aunt and her family in 2005 and compared my Morgan cousins' lives to my own, I was astounded by the differences. Jersey shore crab boils and southwest Louisiana crawfish boils look much the same, but cultural distinctions abound. Casinos, high-rollers, and Boardwalk nightlife characterize Atlantic City's personality as an old New England coastal town. In contrast, the upstart French Cajun country I'd grown up in, with its zydeco-style accordion music, two-step dancing, and ubiquitous tabasco and cayenne pepper sauces, spawned a spicier lifestyle. My upbringing mimicked more my father's midwestern

Indiana heritage than either of the two, but I'd grown to love Cajun customs.

It was the jolly nature of my Aunt Connie, the Morgan matriarch, and my Uncle Nelson who epitomized the primary differences between the Henke and the Bloom sides of my family. In some ways, the Morgans might have been more at home in Louisiana than we were. While Dad read to us Grimm's fairy tales and classic poetry, the Morgans relished retelling stories of their family's adventures, even when those exploits bordered on the absurd. In fact, they took great delight in the absurdities. Nothing illustrates this dissonance between our families better than the story of the spider monkey.

"He resided in splendor near the back door where I had to pass him every day with baskets of clothes to be hung out to dry." Aunt Connie, Mother's younger sister, told this story when Tim and I gathered with more than a dozen cousins and family members for a crab boil in Atlantic City in 2005. "He always acknowledged my presence with a handful of feces to fling at me as I raced by." Aunt Connie was retelling the story, her children and grandchildren leaning in to hear again the narrative that had reached mythic proportions in the Morgan family.

"Mom, what do monkeys eat?" This question posed by my young cousins and their friends one day many years ago should've put their mother on notice, but Aunt Connie was the kind of woman who took a lot in stride.

"I don't know. Bananas, maybe." She thought that was the end of it, until she learned about the spider monkey the kids had befriended in what they called the boondocks, "where all manner of discarded stuff stimulated their imagination," Aunt Connie said, "It was the dump, really. And any monkey you find at the dump is *not* a good monkey!"

Regardless, my cousins brought the monkey home and my Uncle Nelson helped construct a cage for him, which the monkey escaped from almost daily. They eventually rehomed the monkey with an Italian haircutter in town, who thought the creature would add some flair to his salon. The last Aunt Connie and Uncle Nelson heard, one night the monkey escaped the chains that held him to a tree constructed in the center of the salon and destroyed his new home.

"We didn't investigate the future of the monkey after that, though the barber told us he'd given the monkey to his father." I can still hear Aunt Connie's rasping laugh at this point in the story. "Yeah, I just *bet* he did."

Our visit to Atlantic City was the last hope in my quest to discover details of Mother's youth. Since Dad's death in 1994, Aunt Connie was the only living relative who had known my mother in her youth. Breaking the silence with the questions I asked my dad in 1982 at Graceland Cemetery had been the first, and hardest, step I took. Prior to this, I'd been on my own to learn anything useful.

In the mid-70s, amid child-rearing insecurities, I did a bit of tentative research into schizophrenia. At least two factors complicated my search. Browsing the card catalog at the downtown library in Lake Charles for medical information was clumsy and ineffective. Besides, there were scant conclusions about the origins and effective treatment of schizophrenia. I was still several years younger than my mother had been at diagnosis, and there was something ominous about reaching those thirty years. What I needed to know was the likelihood of inheriting the disease. Even more troubling was the prospect of inflicting "bad genes" on my children, who were quite young.

What I found was a novel about a sixteen-year-old girl who spent three years in a mental hospital after being diagnosed with schizophrenia. This was a scenario I could relate to. *I Never Promised You a Rose Garden* describes the girl's imaginary world, created from psychotic delusion, and the heroic efforts of a psychiatrist to save her. I learned later the book was a somewhat fictionalized account of the author's life (Joanne Greenberg), and that the author and the novel would generate a great deal of skepticism about the accuracy of both the diagnosis and the "cure." I took heart in dissimilar behaviors during her "journey back from madness," not yet confident I wouldn't make my own journey someday. More disastrous, if schizophrenia were to overtake my children, it would be all my fault. The anxiety these thoughts introduced couldn't be articulated. It seemed best to stuff down my fears; better not to think about them.

In the 80s, I read *My Mother's Keeper*, by Tara Elgin Holley, to learn what it might be like to not only have a schizophrenic mother but to be responsible for her care. In the 90s, I read *Motherless Daughters*, by

Hope Edelman, to learn how other daughters coped with mother loss, but mothers lost to insanity initiate a unique sort of grief. No one's experience was just like mine. In *After Schizophrenia: The Story of My Sister's Reawakening After 30 Years,* Margaret Hawkins describes witnessing her sister, Barbara, spiral into undiagnosed and untreated schizophrenia, then becoming Barbara's guardian after her parents' death. Her book, and conversations with my cousin Mary, who grew up with a schizophrenic mother (Mother's younger sister) led me to wonder if I was more—or less—fortunate to have been separated from my mother. It's impossible to know.

More recently, I read *He Wanted the Moon* by Mimi Baird whose father Dr. Perry Baird suffered from schizophrenia and was institutionalized off and on a full decade earlier than my mother's first hospitalization. Dr. Baird wrote his own story for his daughter to discover decades later. In 2021, Mimi was kind enough to speak with me on the phone about our common experiences, the code of silence we were both bound by. She encouraged me to tell *my* story.

I joined a Facebook group in 2019 called "Motherless Daughters Support Group," hoping to meet daughters from whom I could learn about making peace with mother loss. What I found were women who still grieve viscerally months, years, and decades after their mothers' deaths. Many women haven't—can't—move on. Surely the mothers they lost wouldn't want them to wallow in the sort of grief that prevented them from carrying on a legacy of loving others, but I had to admit I just didn't understand.

"Are you *serious*?" I wanted to ask the woman who couldn't bear to have a Christmas tree in her house for her two young children to enjoy because Christmas was her mother's favorite holiday. In response to another online poster, I wanted to shout, "You can't get out of bed on your mother's birthday, four years after her death? What's *wrong* with you?" I read some posts to my husband, stunned by vitriolic rants about fathers dating again or about an insensitive comment by a sister or best friend they will never speak to again.

"Why do you keep reading them?" Tim said, "Just drop out of the group."

"It's kind of interesting," I mumbled. Despite my callousness toward what I judged to be exaggerated pain, I felt compelled to read on, pulled into their posts like rain into a dry gulch. These women all had something I lacked: memories of their mothers.

I don't have a loving message in a mother's cursive tattooed on my wrist or her fingerprint immortalized in a locket. I can't hear her voice or smell her cologne on the blanket she left behind. I don't remember the feel of her fingers combing through my hair or a finger tracing tears on my cheek. I can't answer when someone asks, "What was your momma's favorite song?" Or "What did your mother always cook for you when you were sick?" What surprised me more about the posted questions I couldn't answer was the fact that so many—dozens and dozens—*did* answer them, with enthusiasm. And I was jealous. We're all motherless daughters, but these women inhabit unknown territory. I've moved on in what I consider satisfactory ways, and I have marvelous memories of people and events that enriched my life. Yet when someone posts, "Momma was my best friend," I tear up.

I turned to my Aunt Connie for information because I knew she was the last living link to my mother's childhood. We traded a few emails in which she shared a few facts about their family history.

"We were brought up in a most puritanical atmosphere," Aunt Connie wrote, early in 2005. She insisted the four Bloom children both adored and respected their parents. I don't think my father was convinced that Mother shared this sentiment; at least *he* didn't share it. I don't know how well he knew them, though. Aunt Connie also admitted that because she was so much younger, she and Mother didn't travel in the same circles, and she couldn't provide many specific stories, either.

After describing a lifestyle of ease and association with the "right" people, she added a comment about my mother's attitude, "Wealth was never a priority for her, but moral goodness was." I wasn't sure what to make of these contradictory statements and wasn't sure what it said about my mother's character. After a few months of off-and-on communication with Aunt Connie, a piece of good fortune landed in my lap.

Tim was planning a business trip to Pennsylvania,

and he suggested I accompany him and make the drive over to Ventnor, just outside Atlantic City, for a brief visit with Mother's remaining family. Aunt Connie and my cousin Linda were both eager to reconnect.

"Please come!" Linda said, "Mom will be so glad to see you!" I'd seen Linda several years earlier when my brother's family lived in Maryland on temporary assignment. When we visited Jon's family there, he arranged a dinner with Linda and her sons, who lived nearby in Virginia.

I hadn't been to New Jersey in 40 years, though; not since my mother's death, and I was a little hesitant. I didn't know these people well, despite being related. However, I recognized a once-in-a-lifetime chance to become acquainted beyond the annual Christmas card exchange.

We drove straight to my cousin Kim's house from the airport for dinner with my aunt and uncle and a host of cousins and their families. They welcomed us with a huge spread of food at the home that had housed two generations of Morgans. Meeting them after so long a time was gratifying, but I felt awkward and a bit dazed with family overload. For two days, we heard stories of their families' escapades: stories of my cousins finding and adopting a troublemaking, shit-slinging spider monkey from the dump, finding a dead body once in the ocean and being instructed by the police to go through his pockets for identification, stories pulled out to entertain long-lost relatives. These were my aunt's people, and by extension *my* people. It seemed a homecoming, but it was unfamiliar all the same.

I've sadly forgotten some of the names and stories. What remains is the vague impression of family life that is so unlike my quiet, somewhat controlled upbringing as to seem foreign. My husband recognized the lively storytelling and chaotic meal setting from his own, though, with five siblings and ever-present, though smaller, extended family. He was so taken with it, he's told the story of the spider monkey to everyone we've ever mentioned this trip to for the past fifteen years. It reminds him of the baby squirrel he and his brothers kept in their bedroom until it bit him so hard on the web between his thumb and forefinger that he slung it out the window and told his siblings it escaped.

The Morgan family exuded a sense of playfulness and deep regard for each other, aside from the occasional good-natured verbal spars. I tried to imagine my mother in the midst of such a family, but I couldn't. Unfortunately, none of the stories included my mother. Despite that, the easy banter and evidence of shared love almost—*almost*—made me feel as though I belonged. It still seems a family I have no claim on.

It took me too long to build the courage to reach out to Aunt Connie in the first place, and I tried to soak in the personalities around me and listen to their stories. I'm sure I wrote in a journal or notebook, because that's my habit when I travel somewhere new. I know better than to trust my memory. The notebook is lost, however. I suspect I tossed it unintentionally, along with ones I deemed unimportant during our last move to Texas.

At the end of the weekend, I had to face the fact that I'd learned as much as I ever would about my mother's childhood. I gained a great deal more, though. While I didn't—and don't—quite feel a part of the same family, I sense there are deeper similarities than I'm able to recognize. We share some measure of DNA, and schizophrenia doesn't taint it all.

My cousin Linda's husband, George, generously supplied me with copied photos of my mother and other family that Aunt Connie had in her possession, and he scanned others onto a DVD. These have become part of my meager but cherished collection. He also scanned pages of the family Bible that all supposed were lost.

Aunt Connie was delighted when presented with the Bible. "I thought it was burned with the photo albums!" Her mother (my grandmother) had traveled out west with her own mother for a year after high school instead of college and had cherished reliving her youth by perusing the photo albums she'd kept from their travels. "We thought Mary burned this Bible along with all those albums," Aunt Connie said. Mother's youngest sibling, Mary, also diagnosed with schizophrenia, had lived with her children much of the time at my grandparents' home, where the family heirlooms were stashed.

A family legend insists that my grandmother, whose maiden name was Taylor, was a descendent of former president Zachary Taylor, and that this family was descended from a Peter Brown who had landed in America via the Mayflower in 1620.

Handwritten notes at the front of the Bible trace the Taylor family from this supposed ancestor, with occasional birth dates and names of wives and children through 1814. According to the last note by a presumed relative, L. A. Taylor, "These are records of my maternal grandparents and their family taken from their family Bible." The accuracy of the claims is questionable, but who am I to doubt? From what I've gathered, there are so many people in the US who claim Mayflower connections that nearly everyone alive today is related.

"Mother was so proud to be a Mayflower descendent," Aunt Connie said, as she sat up taller in her wheelchair. "You've got some pretty famous relatives," she said with a grin, "but we try not to let it go to our heads." Her eyes sparkled.

It seems a harmless fiction, and I loved hearing Aunt Connie tell it so animatedly. Every moment of her storytelling seemed a window into the history she shared. I invented a vision of my mother in front of me, making use of similar mannerisms and expressions. These were the last puzzle pieces I expected to receive about my mother's early years.

By the time our visit ended, we'd walked down streets and in front of houses Mother lived in as a child and walked the Monopoly neighborhood—Marvin Gardens, Park Place, Tennessee Avenue, and so on—in an entourage that included Aunt Connie in her wheelchair and the oxygen required to combat emphysema. We'd enjoyed the crab boil around long folding tables in the backyard. Some of the cousins' children performed a play to entertain us. And we pored over photos and the family Bible. It was a lot of activity for a couple of days, charged with a fragile sense of connection. The link was short-lived, as Aunt Connie died the following year, and only occasional communication continues with the cousins. But our parting words and hugs will remain in my memory.

"You've given me back my sister!" Aunt Connie exclaimed as we left their home on Sunday. There were tears in her eyes as I hugged her goodbye.

"You've given me back my mother," I countered.

In 2008, a few years after our trip to New Jersey and during my second semester of teaching high school, Karen asked me to spend my Spring Break helping her recover from shoulder surgery. I was neck-deep in obsessive lesson-planning, so I lugged a 30-pound canvas bag full of textbooks with me. Her husband, Dale, worked nights and slept most days and was hard of hearing. Karen's recovery was going well, and aside from a sling and sore shoulder, we were on our own. I hijacked Karen one afternoon to visit Mother's grave with me.

Although I'd lived twenty-six years in Lake Charles, I'd only been to Graceland Cemetery twice before. Once was the day of my mother's burial, when I was thirteen. In 1982, I'd brought my father there. That year, after two more decades, I brought my sister Karen and a bouquet of silk flowers. I had only a vague sense of where to find Mother, and Karen had no idea. A cemetery as eclectic as Graceland is disorienting with its brick and stone mausoleums, cement slab edifices and marble—endless marble headstones, statues, crosses, and carvings.

"I don't have a clue where her grave is," Karen said with a shrug, "Haven't been here since we buried her." She was eighteen when Mother died.

Karen waited in the car while I hunted among the headstones, protecting her sling-clad shoulder and vulnerable knees with their synthetic parts.

"It's in this eastern half," I insisted, "I know it."

Every time I returned to move the car further down the path, she shook her head. "Can't help you." The day was warm, not unusual for March in Louisiana, and I'd lowered the windows and found slivers of shade to park her in.

I searched a good while without luck, going over and over the same ground, becoming friends with the residents I circled, recognizing old Lake Charles names: Thibodeaux, Assunto, Mayo, and Huber. They seemed to welcome me to where their ancestors had been buried for over a century. I also took a tour along the property's fence line, where Karen said they'd buried her stillborn daughter in 1969, marked with a simple, small cement slab inscribed with her name. I didn't find Mary White, but a lot of the cement pads used to mark infant graves were eroded and unreadable. After almost an hour of looking, I hadn't found Barbara Henke.

"I'm sorry," Karen said, "I know you had your heart set on finding it." She'd waited patiently in the car, her fair skin growing pink from the sun shining through her open window. In fact, she was quieter than she would otherwise have been. She left me to my search, without help or hinder.

"This was one of the few things I wanted to do while I was here."

"The cemetery office closed years ago," she said as we drove back to her house, "Why don't we look on the internet? Maybe there's a cemetery map online."

There wasn't anything online but the cemetery address. The phone number listed was disconnected. "What about the library? Wouldn't they have some records?"

"There's a genealogical library downtown," Karen said. "Let's try there."

Within an hour, we'd located a map and a section identifier for Barbara Bloom Henke at the library. Back at Graceland, we searched—both of us this time—through section G, row 4, for another fifteen minutes before we found it. I realized I'd never have found it from memory. Her headstone was indeed on the eastern half of the cemetery, but I didn't remember it being on the fringe, on the last populated row of Graceland. Though there were plenty of burials after 1966, they sold few plots after that date. The city took over the cemetery soon after and used it for burials in family-owned plots ever since. The newer, more spacious cemetery on the southwest edge of town has been the site of more frequent burials in recent years, including those of most of our deceased family members.

There isn't anything remarkable about Mother's headstone—a marble marker with her name, her birth and death dates, and a thick cement slab resting on the ground above the coffin. Barbara Bloom Henke rests next to John McElroy Eckhart, our former pastor's father. It hadn't ever occurred to me before to regret that we buried her among strangers.

I believe in life after death, and I don't believe my mother is stuck in eternity with these people she never met, yet I'm uneasy knowing that she is out of the way, in someone's unwanted burial plot, unvisited. None of her family visited there, even though Aunt Connie once came through Lake Charles on her way from New Jersey to her winter home in Arizona. If my father ever made the drive across town to Graceland without me, I wasn't aware of it.

It pleased Karen that we found the grave, because it pleased *me* to find it. Once we had, I wasn't sure what I intended. I took pictures—some close and some farther away—to ensure I could find it again. I arranged the flowers in the vase anchored at the foot of the cement slab, then we drove away.

The next morning, after I'd said my goodbyes, given hugs and kisses, and loaded up the car, I headed again for Graceland. I needed to come alone.

It was another warm and humid morning with fresh dew working its way into the atmosphere. The silk flowers had shifted in their vase overnight and drooped over the edge. Circling the grave, I straightened the flowers and tried to see the scene as through a viewfinder on a video camera. *This is what I see from this angle, and from here...* and here. I whispered to my mother as I moved. "I'm here. I found you." The words felt awkward, as though they might mean more to her forty years beyond her passing than in the dozen tortuous years before. "I'm sorry I didn't come before." It may have been the first time I'd contemplated all that Mother had lost, and not what her illness had cost me.

The previous day when we were at Prien Memorial Gardens in south Lake Charles visiting the graves of our father and grandparents, Karen said, "I sometimes think Dad is watching over us from heaven. I like to think he does that."

I've never bought into the sappy "angels watching over us" sentiments portrayed in books with seraphic cover art. But I didn't snicker at Karen's statement. Instead, I said, "That's a nice thought."

As I stood at Graceland that last morning, looking over the sea of marble and cement representing generations of mothers, fathers, sisters, and brothers, I could almost envision my mother among a horde of transparent beings, watching. Seeing me straighten the flowers with a loving touch. Smiling at me the way she's smiling at Karen in the photograph from 1947, right after Karen's birth. She's so proud of her child in that photo. Dad's sitting next to her and they're both staring at my scrawny sister, their firstborn, with adoring eyes. Those were the eyes I'd always hoped to see focused on me. For the first time, an invented version of my mother as she was meant to be allowed me a picture of her maternal pride in her youngest child.

Southeast Louisiana Hospital
Henke, Barbara
Hospital Number 201

Progress Notes

April 28, 1957:

The writer received a visit from the husband of this patient on this date to discuss her condition. After he had had an opportunity to air his feelings, it was agreed that the family would be allowed to make the actual transfer of this patient to Central Louisiana State Hospital; that the husband would be allowed to take her home after we had made all the arrangements and got the necessary permissions for the transfer and then he would take her from their home to Central Louisiana State Hospital.

May 18, 1957:

The patient is this date placed on Discharge Status by reason of transfer to Central Louisiana State Hospital, Pineville, Louisiana. A copy of her commitment papers and receipt for her transfer were mailed May 17, 1957, a copy of her receipts to be returned for our records. A copy of her case summary was mailed April 12, 1957.

XIX
Eyes Wide Open

In the spring of 2008, a pair of yellow finches made their nest in the trees at the edge of the park where my friend Helga and I walked a couple of times a week. On several crisp mornings, the finches put on a lively show near the cars parked just west of the park road. They flapped aggressively at the bird they viewed in the cars' rearview mirrors. Again and again, they dove, making runs at the mirror with each dive, wings outstretched to their broadest, scariest pose. Bright yellow feathers fluttered in the sun, reflecting sunlight from both the sun and the mirrors. They chirped and chattered, warning intruders to stay away from their nest. We stood perhaps twenty or thirty feet away as we talked and cooled down after walking our three miles. Until I pointed the birds out to Helga, she didn't see or hear them.

Another day, I was transfixed by a couple of other park-goers, but I didn't want to interrupt Helga's story. When she paused, I leaned over to whisper, "What do you think they're doing here?"

This was the fourth or fifth time I'd seen these men at the park. One was tall and lean, with a beard and thinning pate, in jeans and T-shirt, holding a sheaf of papers. He gestured enthusiastically as he talked. *He's a talker, too.* The other man, with neat hair, slacks and a sport shirt, listened intently and nodded without speaking. This was the pattern: they talked for about fifteen minutes and then they left, the thin one in his battered light blue Chevy panel van, the other man in a nondescript sedan—a Camry, I think.

Helga was startled. "Who?"

"*Don't look!*" I hissed. When we were out of earshot, I said, "Those two guys on the bench back there, they've been here the past couple of weeks. What do you think they're doing?"

I'd imagined the thin man was proposing a business deal or that he was an evangelist or the ex-husband of the other man's wife. Maybe one was a hit man or a drug dealer. Anything was possible.

Helga and I had been walking at this park for so long we knew the regulars: the paunchy Pakistani man who thundered, "Good morning!" the older man with the toy poodle named Nicky, the frail gentleman in the bike helmet who rode his single-speed bike around us with a ding of his bell, and the pair of ladies who parked their black Jaguars side by side and walked in their look-alike dark leggings. It was clear these men who talked on the park bench hadn't come for exercise.

"What men?" Helga said.

I was astonished. How could she not have seen them? I told her my theories. "What do you think?" As we rounded the next bend, she peeked back and shrugged.

"I don't know," she said, "I hadn't noticed them."

We'd circled this half-mile track more than four thousand times in ten years. During those two thousand miles of walking, we shared more words than many married couples. Words about our children, our deepest fears and greatest joys: four marriages, one divorce, one broken engagement, one daughter's move to Japan and then Great Britain, one pregnancy, my husband's layoff, and her husband's retirement. We talked about politics, religion, book plots, and our assessment of current events, most of which we agreed on.

Despite all we shared, we have different strategies for absorbing our world. Helga hones her ideas in her listener's ears; I do most of my thinking in quiet moments. Spoken words can distract my thoughts; for Helga, visual stimuli are distracting. I understand and appreciate this about her, but it surprised me when she sometimes missed what lay ten yards beyond her feet. Her words could wash over and around me while I was lost in observation of rain puddling in the dips of asphalt track or the huddles of geese that honked their hellos to each other around the park's central pond. It's reminiscent of lying on the floor as a child and studying my mother through the crack under the bathroom door or watching her cut fabric into pieces to see what she'd do next. Threaten someone with the sewing shears? Pour bleach in our lemonade? You could never tell. Whether from curiosity or a sense of lurking danger, I keep one eye on my surroundings.

Experiences of pondering my mother's erratic behavior spawned a penchant for inventing the backstory for perfect strangers and to imagine myself in another life. They compelled me to expect and prepare for what might happen next. Sometimes it protected me from danger.

Tim's become accustomed to the stories I tell him about the people sitting at the next table in restaurants or the young mother and child sitting behind us in the airport. I'll study the man pacing up and down the long hall in front of our gate and listen to his one-sided conversation on the cell phone clipped to his belt buckle and connected by a dangling earbud wire. "He'll miss his meeting in Spokane," I murmur to my husband, who's intent on his email and responds with a distracted "Uh huh."

My husband's accommodating, but he just nods at my observations without engaging. He's got his own way of observing the world. His strategy entails leaving the well-worn trail and traipsing off on a deer path. He tromps through the sticker-clad brush and woods of the county park near our home to find evidence of feral hogs. Or he tramples over the faint trails our dog pulls him through to pick up the trash left by kids who partied, away from the walkers and runners who frequent the mulch and cinder paths. This strategy is an assault on my senses, too much to process at once. I prefer staying on the trail, where I can think my own thoughts and observe incremental, subtle changes through the seasons, from purple verbena to Indian blanket to Black-Eyed Susan and Mexican Hat wildflowers. I talk to the fawns and bunnies. They run at the sound of my voice, but what fun to be surprised by them!

Paying attention and staying open to what came next were habits that paid off in my career too. Attracted to analysis and making sense of data, I spent a good bit of my career engaged in scientific discovery. It all began with the chemistry set I got when I was ten, but my passion for discovery had just begun.

When I was a junior in high school, I enrolled in the Special Chemistry class. It was the equivalent of an Advanced Placement class in the early 1960s, a program that hadn't reached Lake Charles yet. The course spanned two class periods and included a mere handful of girls. We did real-life labs that sometimes flopped miserably, requiring that we troubleshoot the variables and rework the hypothesis. We couldn't always tell what we'd end up with, whether or not the labs worked. Sometimes, the product was more interesting or more useful than expected. There was always something to learn, and I loved it.

Karen's first husband, Don, was a blood bank technologist at Lake Charles Memorial Hospital. When he learned I was looking for a part-time job during senior year, he suggested the open position in the hospital lab for a weekend clerk. After a couple of years of handwriting lab results and delivering reports to patient charts, I enrolled in the Medical Technology program at McNeese State. The orderly, organized laboratory environment suited me. Plus, patients' lives sometimes hinged on my accurate and timely transfer of lab results to caregivers, and that appealed to my need to feel valuable.

It's hard to know how much of my science career was guided by a children's chemistry set or a natural sense of curiosity, but science has shaped who I've become. By the time I got my B.S. in Biology/Medical Technology in 1976, I was already a wife and the mother of two. I'd worked nights and weekends during my college years, while pregnant with both children, and began full-time work as soon as I returned from my second maternity leave and passed my Medical Technology certification exam.

My med tech career continued off and on for the next twenty-odd years in three states and through research, clinical, blood bank, and hospital laboratories. My position as a research technologist in the 1990s blended the best of my skills with the most valuable of goals—discovering key factors in the development of a variety of cancers. But my heart broke a few years later when the lab closed. Not long after, I served for a time as a Quality Assurance Specialist at the Tulsa American Red Cross Blood Bank before I left the field altogether in 1994 to pursue a graduate degree in journalism. The intersection between my professional career and that of my parents hasn't escaped my notice. I first majored and worked in science, as my father had done and as he encouraged. My second degree was in journalism, just as my mother's was. Circumstances cut her career aspirations short, but I hope I've made the most of my own opportunities, maybe for the both of us.

Professional pursuits only went so far in satisfying my passions, though. Still aware of my losses as a child, I was drawn to children and youth in danger of life-altering neglect—children with barely "good enough" parents or worse. Multiple people, many of them mothers, had shown me compassion and care through my childhood, demonstrating how critical it is for adults to promote the well-being of *all* children. As a result, I developed empathy for children in distress and a desire to give of my time to benefit others.

Somewhere a Child is Crying, by Vincent Fontana, published in 1973 (the year our son was two years old), opened my eyes to an issue I'd never considered: violence against children at the hands of their parents or caregivers. It rocked my idealized perception of parenthood and mother-child bonds like nothing else had. The familial relationships I'd observed so far were nothing like those described in Fontana's book. My father was a quiet and patient man, and the thought of him stringing a toddler up by her wrists and beating her raw with a belt was so far out of the realm of possibility as to make it seem fictional. Yet I came to believe it was possible, and that knowledge had a profound impact.

When a four-year-old boy I'll call Bennie came to the emergency room of the hospital where I worked, our son Marc was about the same age. Bennie had a mop of blond hair similar to Marc's and carried the same sweaty-boy smell. He didn't fight or need to be restrained, as most youngsters did when I drew blood from their arms. I never saw the color of Bennie's eyes.

At the time, most hospital personnel had access to the patient charts in the wards, which comprised bulky paper files. Nurses protected them somewhat, but as hospital staff, I had reason to read chart notes relevant to lab analyses and wasn't bothered by the floor nurses if I scanned them.

According to Bennie's chart, there had been two accounts of his injuries: one from his mother and one from his father. "Patient either fell from the back step of his home, or he fell from a living room sofa," his admitting physician noted on his chart, "No bruises or other injury consistent with either explanation is obvious. Will rule out sudden loss of consciousness because of undiagnosed condition." Before the true cause of his coma could be determined and before he regained consciousness, Bennie died.

This incident, more than any other, galvanized my efforts over the next forty years to advocate for troubled, abused, or neglected children. I'd heard of Parents Anonymous and wanted to form a similar group in Lake Charles, but I had no expertise as a community organizer, and this effort didn't take off. Determined to gain the skills I lacked, I spent the next few decades learning how to be effective as a project planner and a volunteer.

We moved to Port Arthur in 1978, and I

connected with the local Child Protective Services office. Volunteers worked together to form a group for mothers who neglected or abused their children, some of whom still lived with their mothers. We invited speakers to meetings: pediatricians, nutritionists, teachers, and child development experts. Sitters provided child care in another space so moms could bring their kids, and sometimes whole families took part in craft activities or outings.

Each volunteer was paired with a mom, and that's how I got to know Carol. For over a year, I transported Carol and her children to meetings. Carol *wanted* to be a better mom, but I suspect she suffered from severe depression, and she had absolutely no support system. I invited her kids to our church's Vacation Bible School and provided transportation; I included her family in our Christmas caroling event that December. Her children contacted me off and on for months afterward, but eventually her son moved in with his father, the girls grew up, and I lost track of them. I couldn't help seeing myself and my siblings in this scenario and imagining how life would have been different living with a mom who was imperfect to the point of neglect, even if she tried to do better.

Over the next ten or fifteen years, I volunteered with child protection agencies in Texas and Oklahoma. When we moved to Tulsa a second time in 1989, I continued my advocacy by volunteering with a county program to mentor a girl in foster care. Her father—also her soccer team coach—had molested her and was convicted of lewd behavior toward the guests at her ninth birthday party, the other girls on her team. They effectively gave him a life sentence and her mother's parental rights were severed.

For three years, I mentored the girl and drove her each week from her school to a counselor's office and back to her foster home—a 100-mile trek for me—and sometimes for outings or visits to our home. This child was a prime example of my psychiatrist friend Erv's insistence about resilient children, even without "good enough" parenting. Her father was abusive, and the courts determined her mother negligent in protecting her. Her mother, who I suspect had also been abused, seemed to care, though. With state support and excellent foster placements, her daughter managed the sunniest disposition possible, given the circumstances.

My desire to meet the needs of others didn't end with at-risk children, however. I've always been interested in the welfare of those marginalized by limited resources, both physical and emotional. In 1996, I had an opportunity to join a medical mission team with fellow church members to Guyana, South America. The goal was to assist medical personnel at the Public Hospital in Georgetown, and my technical skills would be a distinct asset. When asked to join the team, I agreed without hesitation. Geography not being my best subject, I thought Guyana was in Africa, but that's another story.

My first mission trip to Guyana allowed me to

use my medical technology expertise to help resolve ongoing technical problems at the public hospital's laboratory. My specific mission proved successful, and the broader experience of being part of a mission team was so gratifying that I accompanied two more trips to Guyana in 2000 and 2005. The last was a mental health mission, the long-held hope of our mission director, child psychiatrist Dr. Erv Janssen (who promoted the "good enough" parenting model). A few months before, I'd joined a team from our church for a community education series about domestic violence. Erv thought a presentation on that subject would fit into the mental health trip, as domestic violence is rampant in Guyana. Our mental health seminar for psych nurses would convene at the country's only psychiatric facility.

What confronted us at the Ft. Canje Psychiatric Hospital was disheartening, even more so than the Central Louisiana State Hospital, where my mother spent the last years of her life. Both institutions are of similar vintage, and both had experienced similar decay, yet Ft. Canje continued to house mostly untreated and forgotten patients while there are no long-term residents at Central State today.

Sixteen men shared each long, narrow dormitory in the men's ward. Their beds consisted of dirty and split mattresses (if they were lucky enough to have them at all) sitting atop 12-inch cement pedestals rising above the concrete floor. No walls. No partitions. Each resident had a TV tray at the end of his bed, but there was otherwise no furniture in the hall. Men splayed face up and face down, mostly unmoving, as though they had nowhere else to go ... and they didn't.

"Conditions at Ft. Canje are deplorable," Erv had warned before the trip, but we were still shocked.

"Guyana was considered the 'Jewel of the Caribbean' in terms of psychiatric services in the 1960s," he said. It surpassed most American psychiatric care. "They used a more holistic approach to care than is evident in the US." The combination of useful physical occupation, talk and behavioral therapy, and pharmacology was more effective than any individual component. Patients came to Ft. Canje from all over the Caribbean for treatment. "More important, there was engagement from the entire community. Patients had support within and without the walls of the hospital, and that was so helpful in their care."

The ornate architecture of the old buildings at the hospital was a testament to a community that once cared about their mentally ill. The Victoria Building, constructed around 1899, was a prime example. It overlooked spacious grounds where patients once played cricket. The field is now overgrown with weeds and brush; the buildings sag as if they've given up hope, too. Great Britain granted Guyana its independence in 1966, the year my mother died. When the British left, according to many Guyanese, "they turned out the lights."

Sadly, the Jewel of the Caribbean became an eyesore. Some attention was paid to maintaining and renovating residence halls, but the status of patient care deteriorated. Despite a staff with great compassion for their charges, there was little useful activity. There were too few overworked and underpaid nurses. Two staff psychiatrists treated over 200 patients.

Attitudes among the Guyanese toward hospital residents had become eerily similar to attitudes in the US "We were told many families left patients at the hospital and pretended they no longer existed," Erv said. When a resident died, often the family didn't even reclaim the body but asked the hospital to mail the death certificate to them. This description both saddened and convicted me.

I'd spent my childhood pretending my mother didn't exist because I feared what her illness said about me or what it predicted for my future. When she died, we did retrieve her body and memorialize her life in a fashion, but I felt only relief at her passing. It wasn't until I was much older that I began to consider my mother's concerns. Dad's account of her illness described her anxiety for me after my birth: the birthmark on my forehead and my bowed legs. He was aware of her fear that he wished her harm, but there may be much he didn't know. In 1953, American psychiatric patients had few effective treatment resources; Guyanese treatments would have been similarly limited. For my mother, and perhaps for schizophrenia patients everywhere, an exile of sorts was the best option. Being banished to an asylum, hours away from your children, thousands of miles from your family of origin, would have been devastating, however. Mother must have feared the thoughts she couldn't control. Perhaps she feared she'd be forgotten by those she loved.

Perhaps she feared being left to die without anyone's notice.

I have no photographs of my mother at Central Louisiana State Hospital, but a humanizing picture of her emerges, though hazy, in her hospital records. Barbara Henke was not just a listless figure on a dirty mattress, as I witnessed in Guyana, and which I might have imagined before reading what nurses and caregivers recorded about her. Mother was sometimes troubled, sometimes a trouble*maker*. Once, she asked to be taken to seclusion because she was "mad at the whole world," and I smile at this expression of human emotion. Isolation could offer a welcome sense of safety she needed. Maybe Mother and I are more alike than I've cared to admit, a perplexing thought.

My experiences at Ft. Canje and at Central State were transient and superficial. At this distance in time, I can't accurately fathom the help or harm they provided to residents, and it wouldn't be fair to assess their efforts. In spite of their failings, both institutions and the residents they've cared for make up integral pieces of my life's puzzle.

Central Louisiana State Hospital
Henke, Barbara
May 1957-January 1966

The only surviving record at this hospital:

Form 86
Name HENKE, BARBARA (WF) DISCHARGED | Case No. 26698
Age 30 | Civil Condition M | Race White | Admitted 5/31/57
Parish Calcasieu | Discharged 6-18-58
Residence Lake Charles, La. | Died
Birthplace New Jersey | Escaped
Previous Att'ks Mandeville, La. | Paroled 5/31/57
Hereditary Hist. None
Religion Lutheran
Correspondent Fred R. Henke, husband, 1609 18th St.,
Lake Charles, La. Phone 6-0924
Diagnosis

Condition at Parole mental- Never in residence
Cause of Death
Disposal of Body

Form 86
DECEASED
Name HENKE, BARBARA WF | Case No. 28216
Age 36 | Civil Condition Mar. | Race White | Admitted 4-15-59
Parish Calcasieu | Discharged
Residence Lake Charles, Louisiana | Died 1-21-66 (Autopsy)
Birthplace New Jersey | Escaped
Previous Att'ks Yes 1957 | Paroled
Hereditary Hist. None
Religion Lutheran DECEASED
Correspondent Fred Henke (Husband) 1609 18th Street, Lake
Charles, Louisiana Phone HE6-0924
Diagnosis #000-x26, Schizophrenic reaction, chronic
undifferentiated type

Condition at Parole
Cause of Death Coronary occlusion
Disposal of Body Hixson Bros. Alexandria, La.

XX
Learning Is the Reward

"It's time to put that away for today," I told Ruth, who hunched over a multi-colored two-foot-high structure and a collection of similar plastic parts that extended from one end of the table to the other. She seemed not to hear me. It was a school day morning in 2012, and her Physical Science classmates had turned in their written assignments and were gathering their books.

"Just a minute," she said, "I'm trying to get this ramp piece to fit, but something's wrong." She studied the instructions and looked back at the piece she was holding.

"Well, the bell's about to ring." The box of pieces strewed out in a dizzying array of purple, orange, yellow, and green, and the Environmental Science class would need the space for their convection current lab next hour.

"Oh, I see! It's upside down." She flipped the orange plastic piece, and voila! The tab fit into the proper slot.

I'd tried to see where she was on the 40-page instruction book, but I couldn't even tell which page she was on, so I was relieved she'd managed it on her own. In fact, ever since we opened the Marble Mania Extreme, a device I hoped would help explain gravity and momentum, I'd been little help. To my surprise, one of the ninth-grade students had taken over the assembly almost as soon as I dumped the 200-plus pieces from the box.

Ruth stood back and looked at her handiwork with a satisfied smile. There were gears, wheels, ramps, and tunnels jutting out at all angles. "It's almost finished," she said.

"You're doing a fantastic job, too. I'm sorry I haven't been any help, but I think you're doing better without me," I said with a laugh. A couple of other students had worked on the project, but they tired of it after a few days. "You might be an engineer someday." She'd also been the student most engaged in the Engino building kits I'd purchased to demonstrate motion and friction.

"I doubt it, Mrs. Airhart." She rolled her eyes and packed up loose parts before moving the project to the counter along the wall behind her.

"Why not? You're good at building things." The bell rang just then.

She shrugged and gathered her books. At fourteen, as the mother of an infant daughter and with no college graduates in her family, her expectations weren't that high.

"I think you'd make a brilliant engineer," I called after her as she left, but the noise of the next class filtering through the door swallowed my words.

Although Ruth didn't pursue an engineering degree, it thrilled me to meet up with her again a few years later at Tulsa Community College, where I was working as the Bioscience Outreach Representative, promoting the college's science programs. She enrolled in basic science courses in my building and stopped by once in a while to check in. "Mrs. Airhart!" she'd yell from the opposite end of a hallway when she saw me, or when she burst into my office to just say hello. "I miss you!"

"I miss you too. How are your classes going?" She was always good for a hug to brighten my day and would tell me about her latest biology exam or her plans to get a degree in psychology. She's a young mom with big dreams; I couldn't be prouder if she were my daughter.

If you'd told me at any point during the first thirty years of my career that I'd one day become a teacher—of high school, no less—I'd have scoffed heartily. After the molecular biology research lab I'd been working in was closed with little warning in 1994, I forged a different career path by getting a graduate degree in journalism and doing some writing. Biological research fulfilled me like no previous jobs had, with unlimited possibilities for scientific discovery; my heartbreak over the lab's closure led me directly to grad school. After graduation and a five-year stint as the *TU Vision* newsletter editor for The University of Tulsa, keeping alumni informed about their alma mater's programs, the siren song of science called to me again. After interviewing alumni, professors, and students at the College of Engineering and Natural Sciences for several years, I was smitten by their passion and decided to pursue an alternative teaching certificate in secondary science.

When I told Tim what I planned, he said, "That's ridiculous! You don't want to do that."

So, of course, I persisted.

I appreciate nothing more than clear goals. Even if I don't have the skills at the outset, I have great confidence that I can learn what I need to in order to accomplish a worthwhile goal. My resolve tested my father's prediction about what I could accomplish, which was confirmed by the pathologist I'd begun my medical technology career with. He'd commented on a job recommendation for me once that I "could do anything I set my mind to." I trusted both assessments, and my attempts to prove them accurate had never disappointed me. At least not until I started teaching high school in 2007, at age 54.

But this story begins seventeen years before.

When we moved back to Tulsa from Dallas in 1989 with World Com after another one of Tim's job transfers, I signed up to be a substitute teacher in area school districts. It was an interim job until I could find something long-term, while I also taught a semester of remedial algebra at the local community college. I only subbed one day—a half day, really—at the Margaret Hudson Program. The organization and the girls it served fascinated me. Classes were held in a Baptist church building, using their Sunday School rooms. The program was a partnership between the Broken Arrow (suburban Tulsa) school district and a United Way funded nonprofit. Instructional materials and teachers were provided by the district, while the nonprofit provided counseling, nursing, and child care for the pregnant or parenting students and their babies.

While I'd been a college student when I got pregnant the first time, I'd still been a teen mom and had faced similar challenges. I hadn't known any classmates at my high school who'd been pregnant, though there were rumors and hints of girls who disappeared from school in disgrace, in the manner that Mom had suggested to me all those years ago. All I'm sure of is that no pregnant students ever *attended* the high school. They were hushed up and off campus, often all the way to Baton Rouge, where young girls of my generation holed up in the late 60s for a few months before returning to their homes without the children they birthed. Attitudes toward "unwed mothers" have changed over the past several decades and have become much more tolerant. Marriage rates for young adults have declined while births to unmarried parents are higher than they've ever been. This acceptance doesn't extend to teenage girls, however. Pregnant students are still ostracized as sluts or worse by their high school peers, many of whom are engaging in sex themselves but haven't yet been caught. Allowing these students to complete high school in a more accepting environment ensured a much higher graduation rate than they experienced otherwise; pregnancy is still one of the most common reasons for dropping out of school. It's also disproportionate among students with few resources.

The Margaret Hudson Program (MHP), which was created with the goal of "helping teen families succeed," intrigued me. I empathized with young women thrust into motherhood before they were ready; I saw myself in their faces and knew their future included hardship. Economic and educational goals would be harder to attain; it would take years for their maturity to catch up with their responsibilities as mothers. As a result, their children would pay the price. As a longtime advocate and mentor for children experiencing abuse or neglect and for young people dumped into the foster care system because of parental failure, I was well acquainted with the possibilities. Without early intervention, these children were doomed to relative poverty along with their parents; at worst, they were at risk of ending up on the wrong end of a state social worker's investigation, or inside a jail cell. This much I knew: they'd lack the assets gained from a secure childhood. MHP provided intervention to help moms graduate high school with supportive teachers and counselors, and modeling of healthy mothering by child-care staff.

In 2001, I began looking for a new volunteer opportunity. My long-term mentoring relationship with a young lady in foster care had ended with her adoption by a local family. When I saw an ad for mentors at the Margaret Hudson Program, I applied. I chose a different student each of the next three school years and met weekly with my mentee over lunch to discuss challenges, to hold or play with her baby if she'd delivered, or to work on a craft project. The bonus was witnessing mother and child bonding from a new perspective and the satisfaction of seeing the young moms' devotion—albeit sometimes clumsy—to their children's needs. Watching a student play peekaboo with her toddler or tweak their toes while I read them a story warmed my heart.

Six years later, when I'd gotten my teaching certificate, it seemed no small coincidence that there was a half-time opening at MHP for a science teacher. It was the only time in my life I felt a divine call to a specific place. The day I walked into the building for my interview, it felt like coming home, as nothing else had. Thus, my high school teaching career began: me feeling a spiritual call to work with these young moms for whom I had great empathy, and the students suspicious of an inexperienced, much older teacher of science subjects they had no interest in. It was a match made in purgatory. I didn't yet know what this leap of faith would cost me, but I leaped with great conviction.

For the next eight years, I analyzed and organized textbook curricula for adaptation to a unique population of students. Classes were small, but I sometimes instructed two subjects to two groups at opposite ends of the classroom simultaneously. I agonized over snarky comments by moody, sometimes hostile hormonal teenagers. I spent dozens of hours—full days *every* Saturday—researching additional resources for lab activities and projects to engage bored students' imaginations. Except for three years, when I added language arts classes to my workload, making eight different subject preps a semester, the district paid me half-time salary. It was exhausting, it was the hardest damn thing I'd ever done, and it was also more satisfying than most any other career. Since then, I've observed through social media that former students have married, completed education or training post-graduation, created loving families, and become responsible adults. Like any parent or mentor of teenaged youth, I despaired of their ever achieving this level of maturity. I'm pleased so many have proved me wrong.

During the years I was struggling to make a difference with our student population, I was keenly aware of my inadequacies. Many students were Latina or Hmong, cultures which encourage girls to bear children at a young age. Some married at sixteen or seventeen. Most of the students were representative of surrounding districts, a few were Black or Asian, but most were white. None of them was shy about expressing impatience with dull lessons.

"When will I ever need to know this?" was a common refrain.

"I really don't know," I responded, "But if you don't learn it, you're limiting your options." This had no effect.

"How do they *know* this?" one student asked, suspicious of the conclusion that the Milky Way is expanding, based on evidence of the ongoing birth of new stars in the galaxy.

"I'm not sure of their methods, but there are many people smarter than I am studying this with specialized tools, and I trust they've done excellent research."

"I don't believe it."

"Well, if it's true," I countered, "it doesn't matter if you believe it or not. It's still true." Neil deGrasse Tyson would be proud.

In the presence of the scientific evidence presented to them, it shocked me they could choose to deny observed phenomena and well-researched data. I'd spent my life searching for evidence—like the existence of a mother who'd once had hopes and dreams as I did—and contemplating what that evidence might mean. It was the way I was wired. It never occurred to me that students could dispute scientific fact, and it led to frustration that sometimes slipped out despite my best efforts. During my second year of teaching, I remarked to one student I'd taught the first year, "I'm so sorry you had to put up with me last year. It was a hard year for me."

I constantly fought for the girls' attention. Because they were at school, I thought learning should be their priority, but it was clear it wasn't. I realize now the changes and unrealistic expectations (many of them mine) they were experiencing. It's amazing that I used to think a biology lesson—even the anatomy of the female reproductive system or the formation of a fetus inside—could overshadow their preoccupations with the everyday realities of pregnancy, childbirth, and breastfeeding.

During my eight years teaching young moms, I blogged about my experiences on a WordPress site, "Learning Is the Reward." The tagline was "No experience is wasted, unless you fail to learn from it." I posted descriptions of the activities and labs I devised to teach concepts. Despite sometimes feeling my efforts were being sucked up into the black hole I was intent on illustrating, I recognized all along that my classroom experiences were educational—at least for me. I loved sharing them online, along with what I learned from them. I'm still convinced every experience in life is instructive.

Occasionally, a lesson met its mark, or an activity engaged imaginations. Like the Marble Mania Extreme, the puzzle resolved by those who had the most to learn from piecing it together. Students from all over campus came by to see the marbles drop, slide, and roll. Watching Ruth show her peers what she'd built and explain how it worked was worth every minute I'd spent laboring over lesson planning for the week. Extracting DNA from strawberries and from students' own cheeks produced the "Wow! Look at that!" I'd hoped for when they observed the stringy, snotty-looking thread of their own genetic material. Letting students emcee the Jeopardy game review for an upcoming environmental science or anatomy quiz gave them a chance to take charge of the classroom for a while, and they basked in it. Those were the days that kept me motivated.

I think I learned more in my eight years working with teen moms than during the previous five-plus decades. For example, a little encouragement is sometimes all that's needed to encourage a young mother—even one as young as thirteen—to make wise decisions for herself and her child. It's more important for parenting students to love their children than to love the subjects I was trying to teach them. It isn't possible to know what effects a teacher has on students until years later, if ever, just as is true for parents. I learned I wasn't called to MHP only for what I could teach my students, but also for what my students could teach me. In persevering, I better learned what kind of person I am, the extent and limits of my abilities.

My son remarked when I told him I was pursuing a teaching certificate, "Gee, Mom. I never know *what* you'll do next." Without deliberate intent, I set examples for our son and daughter about what they could achieve if they continue learning and growing. Marc, a university communications specialist, expands and enriches his life through learning podcast production, practicing ukulele and guitar, and Contra dancing. Kelly, a school district occupational therapist for the past twenty years, recently completed a second degree in mathematics; she subsequently completed a UX Design certificate program and is considering her options. I hope both my children will reach beyond what they think they're capable of, create more meaningful lives, and pass that passion on to my grandchildren.

I've always thought of myself as a fast learner, but, well … maybe not. My disparate careers have become the proof of the confidence given me, first by my father, and later by one supervisor, when they asserted I could be what I wanted and do whatever I chose to do. I thought I needed to know the mother I'd come from, the mother I'd lost at birth, to know who I would be. I was so distracted by searching for both identities that I sometimes failed to acknowledge what life had taught me, who had provided the lessons, and how fortunate I was to have received both.

The puzzle that features my mother and me isn't yet complete. There will be learning adventures in my future, new puzzle pieces to fill the gaps; I'll make room. But I can see now it isn't a two-dimensional picture of a mother and daughter on a cardboard square. It isn't just the image of who we are, DNA included. The puzzle I've been working my entire life to solve is how we've changed each other. My mother shaped me, continues to shape me because of the lens I choose to see her through. She hasn't changed a bit since her death, despite my efforts to reinvent her with eyes that were thirteen, then thirty, then sixty, yet my birth had an undeniable impact on her. I sometimes blamed myself for initiating her illness, but that was an egocentric fantasy; schizophrenia would have found her regardless. And yet her disease didn't erase her as completely as I'd once thought.

My mother's last communication was a letter to my father three days before she died, but which I didn't discover until decades later. I'm startled by the near-poetic quality of her words and the yearning they express to reunite with her family and with a depth that matches my own. This new glimpse of my mother, along with each one that emerges, can define us both in more complex ways.

Pineville, La.
Ward 54
Box 31
Central La. State Hospital
January 18, 1966

Dear Fred,

Had an engaging letter from Mum seems like last week. She sent me a box of writing paper for Xmas. Is always urging me to write.

How are you doing? Know you are thinking of me as I most surely am of you all now.

What a sprinkle we have had last night. Know the falling leaves are holding their breath for a while.

We must have a new cook in the kitchen, a man I believe and sometimes have surprises now. I still like cheese toast and Kellogg's cold cereal.

When are you going to write and come and take me home? We watch T.V. a good bit. Mother said she wanted a by-table tree for Xmas but was outvoted for a large live tree with trimmings. Poor Mum never has a chance.

Love you dearly. Still waiting to hear from you.

Love,

Bobbie

Part III

XXI
Forget Me Not

When we were ten, my friend Janet and I discovered a surefire way to cause a few moments of unconsciousness. We were clever enough to engage in this play at my house, where there wasn't much supervision. Only my sister Karen, a teenager weary of having charge over her baby sister and giggle-prone friends was there, and she ignored us. For several afternoons, we locked ourselves in my bedroom and literally knocked ourselves out. We took turns: one of us was the fainter and one was the catcher. The fainter stood with the backs of her legs brushing up against the bed, then slumped down to her haunches and counted to ten. After the ten-count, she held her breath and jumped upright quickly before her blood pressure had time to adjust.

The result was a sudden blackout.

The catcher's job was to stand in front of the fainter and keep her from falling forward. We didn't need it always, but we were cautious. The fainter fell backwards onto the bed for a few seconds of unconsciousness, a sort of mini nap. The moments after waking were exhilarating.

When it was my turn to catch, I'd study Janet's face and body. Her facial features slackened as she fell back, signaling her loss of consciousness. I leaned forward with my face over hers on the bed, watching her and waiting for her eyes to open, for her to remember where she was. It wasn't possible to take a breath in those few seconds of waiting. My heartbeat and breathing recalled the sensations, and both seemed suspended as I plunged vicariously into brief, blessed unconsciousness with my best friend.

Just as Janet's eyes fluttered open, I glimpsed momentary disorientation before recognition prevailed. We both gasped, then I fell back on the bed beside her while we giggled and reveled in the oddly refreshing sensation of remembering where we were. This was too much fun to keep to ourselves, so we invited a third friend to join us.

"Come see how we make ourselves pass out!" But that afternoon our friend fell neither forward nor back and plunged to the floor between me and the bed, hitting her head on a bedrail on the way down. She wasn't too keen on our pastime and sported a colorful bruise on her forehead for a while, reminding us of our carelessness. At age ten, I didn't have that much memory to lose, but the potential for injury seemed riskier than it had before. I didn't yet know how I would someday guard my memories with deliberate care. They were clues to who my mother was and to who I was becoming. But forgetting can be a mercy too.

A coworker of mine once told me a story about her grandmother, who had Alzheimer's disease and lived in a nursing home. "When Grandad died, Grandma's disease was fairly well progressed," Melinda said, "We weren't sure how she would take the news of his death. She'd been forgetting things and didn't always know who we were, but she always knew Grandad. When he died, we couldn't bring her to his funeral service and tried to break the news to her without upsetting her. She was heartbroken.

"The next day, though, she'd forgotten all about Grandad's death," Melinda said, "When she asked about him, we told her again, as gently as we could, but she grieved like he'd just died. This went on for a couple of weeks until we realized it was just cruel to break this news to her again and again." Melinda frowned and looked away. "We started telling her that Grandad was on his way or that he'd gone fishing. It was hard to say those things at first, because we knew they were lies, but it seemed kinder to let her forget Grandad was dead."

One day, when I was in my fifties, when there was much more to remember, I woke up on my back on a carpeted floor. When I opened my eyes,

I watched the blades of my bedroom's ceiling fan rotate for a bit before I closed them again. I didn't know what day it was. As I'd grown older, my body had rebelled at physical challenges and my language center, once a source of pride, wouldn't easily cough up names or words. Lying there, my first thought was this: Is memory the next piece of ground I'll be forced to give up? I've learned to accommodate loss, but I won't give up memory without a fight.

Within seconds, I remembered with great relief it was a Wednesday morning and my day off. There was a wet cloth in my right hand, and I raised it to press against my cheek where its coolness sparked the memory of the morning, of the aborted walk with our two dogs. I remembered the chocolate lab walking his owner at the end of our street, how our dogs pulled like crazy to meet him, and how their combined eighty-pound weight dragged me off of slippery wet grass to the pavement. I recalled how I saved a face-first plunge with my hands and one knee, which were now raw and bleeding. Then I stood up too quickly from the cedar chest at the foot of our bed to get a bandage for my bloody knee; I was unconscious when the side of my head bounced against the floor.

When Tim discovered I'd passed out and given myself a concussion, he called my doctor without my knowledge, despite my claim I was fine. I didn't even realize he knew my doctor's name. She insisted I go to the emergency room.

"Someone told me you had a fall this morning," her nurse said when she called, "Dr. Willard thinks you should be seen in the emergency room."

"No, really. I've got a slight headache, but I'm fine." Hoping to make greater sense of my memories in written form, I'd begun writing them into essays. I was at my computer when the nurse called and didn't have time for hospital visits.

"Just to be safe," she said.

In 1962, when Janet and I rushed back to my empty house from Oak Park Elementary to make ourselves pass out, my mother was already an old hand at blacking out. She'd sampled insulin shock coma and ECT over a hundred times. ECT's effects on memory and brain function can be profound. In 1958, neurologist Max Fink compared the effects of ECT to those of severe head trauma. While he revised his conclusions in later years, it's interesting that he once likened ECT-induced changes in the brain to concussive head injury. Nevertheless, a great deal of research has provided evidence of memory loss after ECT; the main controversy seems to be whether the loss is permanent.

Although I have few memories of my mother, some are painful to keep, but I won't consciously give any up—good or bad. Sometimes, it seems kinder to forget, as my coworker Melinda discovered. Maybe it's a function of this kindness that I have so few memories available; my forgetting might have begun early and without conscious knowledge. It's possible I just didn't pay enough attention.

My sister Karen learned how to forget some things too. But she recalled enough to tell me about Mother mixing bleach in our lemonade and leaving the lights on in our bedroom through the night sometimes as punishment. "I really don't remember much about those years, though," Karen said, "I hated feeling like I, like we, weren't normal."

I know what she means. When I entered school, I recognized other families weren't like ours, that my mother seemed not to recognize who I was. That craziness was to be feared and that crazy ones should be ostracized, as though mental illness were either moral failure or a stubborn refusal to act normal. I couldn't forget I had a mother who lived in an insane asylum, could I? I couldn't deny it, but I could pretend she didn't exist. Did that mean we were even?

In 1982, when my father and stepmother passed along my mother's hatbox and assorted memorabilia, I was nearly thirty years old—the same age Mother was at diagnosis. The only keepsake I had of her was a ring Karen had given me. The ring isn't valuable, with its tiny chunk of a diamond in the center. It's not pretentious either, with delicate filigreed white gold domed up to a flattened center, where the stone is lodged almost level with the setting. It was too big, but I had it sized and had the thinning band augmented; I still wear it from time to time when I stumble across it in my jewelry box. I don't much like wearing jewelry, though, so after a few weeks, I replace it in my ring holder and forget about it for another good while.

Aside from a ring that didn't quite fit and a black leather scrapbook, the tangible evidence I keep of my mother's existence is stored inside her hatbox: an album with perhaps thirty or forty photos, dating from 1944, when my parents met; a scrapbook of my mother's high school memories; the last letter she wrote to my father; a college typing textbook with her name and a few margin notes inscribed in it; the hospital records from her sojourn at Southeastern State psychiatric hospital from 1953 to 1957; a handful of black-and-white photos; a small collection of papers; copies of vital documents; and the guest book from her funeral service. The hatbox was a gift from my grandmother before my mother's marriage to my father and bears her married initials, "BBH." Barbara Bloom Henke.

Before her death in 1966, I expect my mother had forgotten many of the people and places memorialized in the photos I now study for the stories they might tell. Had she forgotten that she loved to ride horses and boats as a girl, that she played bridge with passion, and that she enjoyed winter trips to her parents' beachside home in Florida as a young woman? Unlike Melinda's grandmother with Alzheimer's, who forgot recent events and remembered life long past, my mother had probably lost both old and new memories.

A few weeks after my concussion, and after the emergency room bills stopped trickling in, I forgot the ballyhoo that surrounded what they diagnosed as vasovagal syncope, or simple fainting after sudden loss of blood pressure. It was embarrassing to admit that after twenty-five years as a medical technologist, up to my elbows in other people's blood and body fluids, I'd fainted at the sight of my own blood. What lingers is the frightening uncertainty of not remembering where I was. I wonder what it was like for my mother to awaken this way day after endless day. She didn't choose schizophrenia any more than I chose to give myself a concussion, didn't deserve her disease any more than I deserve good health. In the end, I hadn't fallen victim to schizophrenia as I'd once feared, a victory not of my winning.

At stake for me now are the decades of memories that make up my life story, which include people and experiences whose influences I couldn't have imagined in third grade when Janet and I rushed home to make ourselves pass out. Some memories are still revealing their value. The thought of losing *any* memory, even ones whose worth is limited to lessons learned, makes me want to gather them up and tuck them all away for safekeeping, somewhere safer than my mother's hatbox. The problem with memories is that as soon as I pull them out to wonder at hidden significance, they become unyielding in my hands, the way Lot's wife became a pillar of salt as punishment for looking back at her home in Sodom, presumably the place she'd lived and loved her whole life. Whether her instinct was born out of anxiety about what lay ahead or what she left behind, I can relate.

Most of my life, I tried to coax a living, breathing mother and a tangible history of our lives out of a collection of random, petrified artifacts and the stories I invented to explain who she was—who I was as her daughter. Artifacts don't surrender truths easily, and there's no one left to ask. Meanwhile, I accumulated memories of my own life through writing the words that seem best to describe them. Those words freeze the moments immortalized in random snapshots that I now guard with the persistent resolve of a daughter determined to remember and to tease out meaning. I'm wary of losing even one.

Because if I lost my memories, who would I be then?

XXII
Late Breaking News

In May 2021, as I was working through what seemed the hundredth revision on this book, and after I'd shared drafts with my husband and children, I received a surprising email from our son Marc. He's the Communications Coordinator for the College of Natural Sciences at the University of Texas in Austin. He has access to newspaper archives that I don't. I'd shared with Marc the dead ends I'd encountered in my search for records of my mother and her family, the Atlantic City Blooms. Since my mother had a degree in journalism and I'd heard she did some writing for the local paper, I'd searched the *Atlantic City Press* online archives and contacted the paper with questions. Nothing came of either effort. I was fully convinced I knew everything I would ever know about my mother, but I was wrong.

"Hi Mom! I found newspaper clips from the *Atlantic City Press* in the 1940s, including about ten articles your mom wrote," Marc said. He included links to mentions of her family, along with those that have her byline. "I was going to wait until Mother's Day, but then it was just too hard to keep it a secret." He'd paid for access to a digital newspaper archive because he knew the articles would be important to me.

The family mentions are mostly society-column fare about a somewhat prominent family in small-town New Jersey in the 1930s and 40s. I commented to Marc that the emphasis on the Bloom family's fashion and community comings and goings were more important than they had been for us, growing up in Lake Charles. Or for Dad, growing up in Indiana. He was evidently aware of the difference in their "stations," which appeared in the history he provided Southeast Louisiana State Hospital at her hospital commitment in 1953.

"I sometimes wonder how my life would have been different if this mother had been my role model," I typed back, "Instead, Dad's more midwestern and modest ethic prevailed."

"I'm glad you didn't end up as a high society lady," Marc responded, "Who knows how I would have turned out?"

Exactly. I've often wondered how life would have been different if Mother hadn't developed schizophrenia. For much of my life, my assumption was that life would have been better or more fulfilling.

But that's not necessarily so. I love my life, just as I've lived it. Now my deepest regrets are for what my mother was forced to endure in her last thirteen years. Schizophrenia snatched a life of promise from her before she was thirty. She couldn't know in the summer of 1943, when she interned at the *Atlantic City Press*, where a few of her bylined stories landed on the front page, that these would be all the clever compositions to survive her.

Marc is the keeper of our family's history as I never was and sees his research in another way. "It's sort of the same rush I get from genealogy, finding a bit of information that few if any living people could know and salvaging it from the wreck of time, giving it a new home in the minds of the living.

"Reading these clips gave me a little glimpse into another time in her life, from an entirely different perspective. Here she is a young woman ... maybe she had big dreams of being an ace investigative reporter. Maybe she loved collecting and organizing information, just as I do."

These glimpses into his grandmother's life—a woman he'd never really considered—generate more questions than he'd ever been motivated to ask. "Was she disappointed her editor assigned her stories that were mostly not big, front-page news? Was it because she was a woman, or because she was so young? Did she yearn to break a city hall corruption scandal or ride along with police and cover a murder suicide, or go on location somewhere exciting and write a travel story?" Marc and I both relate to my mother, cub reporter, as writers and as a complex family member about whom we'll never know everything but who we know just a little better after reading what she'd written.

World War II was in full swing in July 1943, with US and Allied forces launching offensives in Germany (Operation Gomorrah) and Italy that eventually led to Mussolini's arrest. Mother's published pieces expose local wartime issues such as hotel room repairs needed after soldiers visited, worries about coal rationing, and decreased fishing prospects from the city's Boardwalk pier. One headline proclaimed, "Winter Fish Supply Outlook Alarming, Local Dealers Say." A few pieces report on community interests: a newly opened park for children, new rules for service mail, and women's fashion during wartime. "Colors this year will be brighter than ever because the government has commandeered much of the black dyes for use by the armed forces," she reports on July 21.

On the same day US forces bombed Romanian oil refineries and the day before three thousand Romanian gypsies were gassed at Auschwitz, an August story begins in whimsical fashion, introducing a program called Dogs for Defense. "Don't cry because you're a 4-F little dog! You, too, can help win the war. Maybe not in person, but indirectly by contributing to the K-9 Club," Mother writes. She describes the work of canines overseas that contributes to the war effort, backed by the financial support of the

K-9 Club back home. She addresses the possibility of a cat in her reading audience by including a hypothetical letter from a cat named "Toughie Egg Walter," who she assures may join the club as well. The story ends by using what writers call the "donut" technique (my own preferred strategy), by returning to the idea she began with: "So, little dog, you can play an important part in helping win the war. You'll have plenty of company too. Among famous people who have enlisted their dogs to contribute to Dogs for Defense are: President Franklin D. Roosevelt...," and she lists several other prominent names readers would presumably have known.

These discoveries are among the few examples of my mother's words in my possession, and I'm so grateful to have them. I'd long since abandoned my search for new information. Reading newspaper articles she wrote some eighty years ago provides a small window into Barbara Bloom's creative mind as a young adult. They don't express her thoughts, but they illustrate her word choices and language style; her words animate my picture of her. Added to the brief mentions of her and her family in the society section of the same newspaper in the 1930s and 40s—basically just name-dropping—a vision forms of the young woman my mother was at thirteen performing in a Girl Scout play, at sixteen attending a Halloween dance, or writing news copy as a twenty-year-old intern.

I'd sent my husband and children my manuscript draft to give them a chance to make corrections to my remembered events or to clarify their responses to them. What I hadn't realized was that just as I was learning more about my mother from the evidence I found, my family was learning more about me from what I wrote. "Reading these parts of your manuscript was a real gift to me in the sense that I was able to understand the experiences that shaped you and what you went through," Marc said. In much the same way, what my mother wrote, and what she wrote about, helps me understand her in novel ways.

I've been searching for pieces of a puzzle that would show me who my mother was, but that puzzle cannot be separated from her children and grandchildren. We all carry some of her with us, even if we don't know which parts. If I want to know who Barbara Jean was, maybe I don't need to look any further than to those she left behind.

XXIII
Identity

At a recent workshop on the ancient philosophy of the Enneagram, a system that describes nine personality types based on how people perceive the world and manage their emotions, I discovered I was a Six. I also have strong Five tendencies; maybe I'm a 5.5. Add this to what I've already learned through the Myer's Briggs Personality Type Indicator (INFP or INFJ, depending on situation), Five Factor Model of Personality (Strongly Agreeable, Conscientious, and Open to Experience), and the Holland Code (Investigative). You name the self-discovery tool—I've used it. Some of them I've taken several times, just to see if the results change. They mostly don't. Each indicator explains something about why I behave as I do; each of them is a little true and a little false. I'm addicted to taking them, though, and the journey never seems to end.

Called "loyalists," Enneagram type Sixes are motivated by a need for security and often look outside themselves for guidance because they don't trust their own instincts. Our motivations arise from childhood, according to Enneagram experts, and don't change throughout life. Considering the erratic, sometimes dangerous behaviors my mother exhibited, it's no surprise I'm driven by the need for security. Always wary, trust isn't easily given, but when it is, Sixes are loyal. I don't like to think of myself as insecure, because I've developed a thick shell of independence. Some things I trust without question: my image of God, my husband, the credible written word, and science, for example. When I was young, I often hid in corners or behind furniture with a book. Storybook worlds where characters earned their consequences fascinated me; I knew there was something trustworthy within the pages of books.

What nailed my type was this: "Sixes are over preparers. They never want to be caught off guard." Interactions with my mother involved observing what she was doing. I study every situation well before acting; I hate not knowing how to act or react in a situation. Preparing well helps me overcome insecurity, and part of that preparation involves reading and research, as is typical of Enneagram Fives.

As Fives do, I guard my time and energy. I also guard my resources, which is not always an attractive attribute. Oddly, this extends to food. It might be because I resented food restrictions as a teen; to me, food is a symbol of love. I need to have food choices in the pantry and find myself over shopping, in case I'm in the mood for pork and beans, say, or chocolate pudding. While others were busy hoarding toilet paper during the Coronavirus pandemic, I was worrying about running out of frozen green beans. We had enough food to sustain life for months if necessary, but I wanted choices about what to eat. I'd never make a good survivalist.

When I taught high school and college students between 2006 and 2019, I spent far more time preparing to teach than I did teaching. I wasn't secure enough to improvise as some teachers could. I spent Saturdays at my computer, preparing lesson plans and agendas, researching labs, and searching for activities to illustrate topics from our textbooks. Some years, I had only three or four biology students. Most curriculum-based activities made no sense with such a small class, yet those students deserved relevant labs too. The district invested little in lab equipment, so I acquired my own. I bought most grocery or hardware store supplies myself, taking up more of my time and resources. My husband often got drafted to help pull together the wire and alligator clips to create a lemon battery or to screw together the frame for Pedro's gerbil cage. An obsession with preparation kept me alive in the classroom for thirteen years.

My computer's external hard drive still includes impressive accumulations of resources for biology, physical science, anatomy and physiology, environmental science, and English; my collection of materials was the envy of colleagues near and far. To me, those files spelled security and research well done. When we moved to Texas in 2019, I filled three boxes with books of interesting science labs and projects I'd purchased myself over the years and donated them to my former district's science department chair. I kept the other twenty or thirty books related to teaching college English, in case I taught again. Someday I'll let them go, too.

Despite discomfort with the characterization of my need for guarantees of security a la Enneagram, there was comfort in analyzing a snapshot of my character. The need to understand myself and my mother has consumed much of my life, as though my fate depended on hers. I needed to reassure myself that my mother's history wouldn't also become mine, and I treated the evidence I gathered as both prediction and protection. In some sense, I've been trying to lead the life she would've lived if she'd been able, and I've had to invent a life for her from incomplete evidence.

Circumstances marked my character in ways I can't clearly decipher. None of us is captive to a genetic legacy from the day we leave the womb. Our assortment of chromosomes is fixed at fertilization, but even our DNA is subject to epigenetic changes; even twins with identical genetic codes develop individual characteristics. Current research also speculates that trauma can be inherited or transmitted from one generation to the next. Some researchers propose that trauma our parents or grandparents suffered may affect the DNA molecules themselves through methylation or other, as yet unknown, mechanisms. Even without epigenetic effects, each of us will be molded, encouraged, and bruised by our environments—the people and experiences that we encounter. In some ways, we invent our own personalities and our own destinies by choosing to open ourselves to people and events. We can mother ourselves if we have to.

I benefitted from the stable influence of a father who was present, who sacrificed his own comforts and preferences for his three children. My sister understood and supported me without question throughout her life. My brother and sister-in-law now live nearby for the first time in forty years, and we're forging a renewed relationship based on shared memories. My stepmother parented me with grace and humility, and I have three bonus sisters who travelled a considerable section of my journey with me and whom I love. I've learned to appreciate the wisdom I've gained from caring neighbors like Mrs. Davenport, teachers I adored like Mrs. Sims, women of faith like Lois Bekkerus, and respected colleagues like my teaching mentor and friend Linda Jones.

Every mother comes with her own fears and insecurities. The responsibility of shaping a generation of progeny weighs on those who take the duty to heart. Not all do, and this has stopped surprising me. How can a woman with her own scars and disabilities best nurture a child's malleable nature? Most do a "good enough," if not spectacular, job raising children who grow into healthy adults.

Some, like women in the Motherless Daughters Facebook group I joined, keep memories of their mothers as paragons of goodness, forgetting their weaknesses. Death erases inadequacies and obscures prior estrangements or unresolved disagreements.

I look again at that old photograph of my infant self on my mother's chest. She may be distracted, but I'm engrossed by the photographer. One hand is clutching the silk scarf around my mother's neck as I gaze with curiosity at my father's face behind the camera. I'm open to the life that lies before me, whatever it brings. While my mother wasn't able to care for me, my father was. In a sense, he gave up his wife so his children would thrive. It was a choice no parent should have to make.

In another old photo are my dad, my brother, and my sister all together—my childhood family. Like Dad, I enjoyed photography and loved snapping photos with the little Brownie camera I got for Christmas when I was twelve. We'd stopped at a rest stop along the highway, on our way to Indiana to visit my grandparents, when I took this picture of my family sitting at a picnic table in the sun, smiling at my directions to them. Karen in her black cowboy hat, Dad with his arm around Jon, who reached for the other half of his bologna sandwich. This was my family, and I never had reason to doubt that they loved me.

I fantasized about what life might've been like if I'd had a mother through it all and thought I knew what should've happened. I still believe my mother should've been well; no one should have to suffer as she did, lose as much as she lost. But for me?

The curiosity registered on my infant face propelled me to learn from the lessons life had to teach. While I may have lost a mother to schizophrenia, I gained an assortment of others who, through their encouragement, disapproval, or concern, taught me how to make the most of my abilities. Saying yes to opportunities and experiences, some of them downright painful, taught me lessons about the world and how to navigate it well. I wasn't always ready to learn from them, but I recognize the gift in making the most of what I had.

Maybe instead of inventing the mother I wanted, I've invented my truest self. What happened wasn't what I thought I wanted, but it made me who I need to be.

XXIV

2021

Since moving to Texas in 2019, I joined the National Alliance of Mental Illness (NAMI) of Central Texas, with the hope of eventually teaching or facilitating learning sessions with families of those suffering from mental illness. This would be a new area of service for me, and I was apprehensive, but I've avoided confronting my fears regarding mental illness long enough.

In my first eight-week NAMI online class, "Family-to-Family," I learned how today's families navigate mental health resources and how they manage relationships with their mentally ill loved ones. A couple of years later, I took part in a three-week "Families Together" class and volunteered to facilitate future sessions as one who's confronted similar issues of shame and guilt. Most families' stories are heartbreaking.

I'd like to think care for the mentally ill has improved in the fifty-plus years since my mother's death at Central Louisiana State Hospital, but it hasn't changed as much as I expected. Schizophrenia's cause and cure remain elusive, and treatments are unpredictable or ineffective. Families ride the mental illness train blindfolded, much as our family did, and they still must advocate for their loved ones. What we didn't have was a support group such as the ones NAMI organizes or classes to educate us about the nature of schizophrenia that might have helped us achieve a satisfactory balance. These programs could have made all the difference for us, and I hope my time and abilities will help support families who deal with similar circumstances. They needn't suffer in the deafening silence I felt imposed upon me.

The evolution of Louisiana's mental health system and institutional closures track closely with a national emphasis on "community-based," mostly private programs to treat psychiatric patients. Many states have closed public facilities without expanding Medicaid coverage, leaving families without the means to afford treatment for the mentally ill among them. Even when states have adopted Medicaid expansion, there are so few programs available that families struggle to find adequate resources. Without advocates adept at working within scattershot systems, too many mentally ill persons become invisible. And with mental illness diagnoses on the rise, we all suffer the consequences of the traumas the ill encounter: drug and alcohol addictions, homelessness, suicide, lost productivity, and more. We all pay the price.

In 2012, Southeastern Louisiana State Hospital—where my mother was first committed in the early 1950s—was closed. They bussed patients to either Central State in Pineville or Eastern Louisiana Mental Health Systems in Jackson, Louisiana, which doubles as the state's forensic hospital. The closures of smaller Louisiana mental health programs for adolescents or other special needs patients preceded the closure of Southeastern State. Each closure meant a transfer of patients to remaining psychiatric hospitals. Now there are only two in the state.

The 115-year-old Central Louisiana State Hospital complex that figured so prominently in the lives of thousands of Louisiana families, mine included, no longer exists as it did throughout the twentieth century—as a residential community for the mentally ill. The current behavioral health clinic treats patients in day programs and maintains a few beds for overnight stays, but it can hardly be called anyone's residence, as it was after my mother's transfer there in 1957 and for the last years of her life.

The state plans to move the remaining programs within the next few years to a site several miles away, adjacent to Pinecrest Supports and Services Center for adults with intellectual and developmental disabilities. Pinecrest fulfills psychiatric needs for its clients, so it seems the move will create a good partnership and will consolidate state services (meaning, of course, saving money). They will sell the hospital property for development.

If the dormitories, morgue, and administration buildings at Central State are indeed haunted, as ghost hunters seem to believe, the grounds will soon be a ghost town. Pineville city leaders are drooling at the prospect of demolishing structures and converting the over one thousand acres into (taxable) commercial property. One parcel already sold will house a 24-hour convenience store and gas station on property fronting the main highway, something the community badly needs, according to Pineville's mayor. But when the abandoned buildings are no longer standing, I wonder where the phantom residents will go.

When I visited the hospital in 2019, I was haunted by more than imperfect memories of my mother and our tenuous connection in this space. For decades, I grieved what I presumed I lost when she became ill, but I'd just begun to grieve what my mother lost. Being back at Central State after fifty-five years brought into clearer focus what her disease had forced her to give up and the separation she was forced to accept. I gained much more than I'd been willing to acknowledge from what she'd mourned and railed against on these very grounds.

Despite this disconcerting insight, I'm saddened by the thought that Central State will no longer exist. There are no traces of my mother left and no record of her life there, beyond two index cards with admission, discharge, and death dates, along with a few sketchy details about disposal of her body: autopsy in Alexandria and consequent transfer to Hixson Brothers Funeral Home. Yet being on the grounds aroused a diffuse sense of grief for the many anguished souls who'd been committed there, no matter how long they called it "home."

During the writing of this memoir and before the Coronavirus pandemic, I'd hoped to make one more trip to Central State for a tour promised by a hospital administrative assistant I located online, as though walking through empty buildings might put my mother to rest. My husband, Tim, also made contact on my behalf with a couple of individuals from the local historical and genealogical societies who provided bits of informative history. Through these sources, I'd have gleaned more general information about the hospital and its history. But as the year wore on, and COVID restrictions continued, I realized a tour was pointless; I'd already received all the records the hospital kept regarding my mother's care, meager as they were. I would learn nothing more, aside from the insights gained from articulating and organizing my thoughts on paper about what I experienced and who I encountered in my mother's absence.

Instead, I choose to consider the letter Mother wrote mere days before her death as her last words. She expressed a longing for her family that surprised me, despite all she'd suffered. Her description of everyday life as a resident of a now-defunct mental institution was poetic and upbeat. My loving, creative mother was still there somewhere, under the pain and the unfortunate misassembly of brain chemistry and neuronal architecture.

This is where I choose to leave her; this is how I choose to remember her.

Bibliography

The following sources were helpful in writing this memoir and are listed here for readers who would like to know more.

Baird, Mimi and Eve Claxton. *He Wanted the Moon: The Madness and Medical Genius of Dr. Perry Baird and His Daughter's Quest to Know Him.* New York: Broadway Books, 2015.

Ban, Thomas A. "Fifty Years Chlorpromazine: A Historical Perspective" *Neuropsychiatric Disease and Treatment*, 3, no. 4 (Aug. 2007), pp. 495–500.

Bartók, Mira. *The Memory Castle.* New York: Free Press, 2011.

Diagnostic and Statistical Manual of Mental

Disorders, 5th ed. Washington, D.C.: American Psychiatric Publishing, 2013.

Edelman, Hope. *Motherless Daughters: The Legacy of Loss.* New York: Addison-Wesley, 1994.

Erikson, Erik H. *Childhood and Society: The Landmark Work on the Social Significance of Childhood.* New York: W. W. Norton, 1950.

Fink, Max. "Effect of Anticholinergic Agent, Diethazine on EEG and Behaviour: Significance for Theory of Convulsive Therapy." *Archives of Neurology and Psychiatry,* 80, no. 3 (1958): pp. 380-387.

Flax, Jane. "The Conflict Between Nurturance and Autonomy in Mother-Daughter Relationships and Within Feminism." *Feminist Studies,* 4. no. 2 (June 1978): pp. 171 – 189.

Fontana, Vincent. *Somewhere a Child Is Crying: Maltreatment—Causes and Prevention. New York:* MacMillan, 1973.

Francis, Richard C. *Epigenetics: How Environment Shapes Our Genes.* New York: W. W. Norton, 2011.

Freedman, Robert, Sharon K. Hunter, Amanda J. Law, Alena M. Clark, Aquia Roberts, and Camille Hoffman. "Choline, Folic Acid, Vitamin D, and Fetal Brain Development in the Psychosis Spectrum." *Schizophrenia Research*, Apr. 7, 2021, doi: 10.1016.

Fromm-Reichmann, Frieda. *Principles of Intensive Psychotherapy.* University Of Chicago Press, 1950.

Gibson, Alan. "Insulin Coma Therapy." *Psychiatric Bulletin*. 38, no. 4 (Aug. 2014): p. 198. doi: 10.1192/pb.38.4.198.

Greenberg, Joanne. *I Never Promised You a Rose Garden*. New York: Penguin, 1964.

Hawkins, Margaret. *After Schizophrenia: The Story of My Sister's Reawakening after 30 Years*. San Franciso: Conari, 2011.

Holley, Tara Elgin and Joe Holley. *My Mother's Keeper*. New York: Morrow, 1997.

Hor, Kahyee and Mark Taylor. "Suicide and Schizophrenia: A Systematic Review of Rates and Risk Factors."*Journal of Psychopharmacology,* Nov. 2010, 81-90, doi: 10.1177/1359786810385490.

Kirov, George. *Shocked: Insider Stories about Electroconvulsive Therapy*. Self-published: 2020.

Kolker, Robert. *Hidden Valley Road: Inside the Mind of an American Family*. Doubleday, 2020.

"Mental Health by the Numbers." National Alliance on Mental Illness. www.https://www.nami.org/mhstats.

Sadowsky, Jonathon. *Electroconvulsive Therapy in America: The Anatomy of a Medical Controversy*. Routledge, 2016.

---,www.https://theconversation.com/electroconvulsive-therapy-a-history-of-controversy-but-also-of-help-70938.

Saks, Elyn R. *The Center Cannot Hold: My Journey Through Madness*. New York: Hachette,

2008.

"Schizophrenia." *National Institutes of Mental Health*, www.https://www.nimh.nih.gov/health/statistics/schizophrenia.

Watson, James D. *The Double Helix: A Personal Account of the Discovery of the Structure of DNA*. London: Weidenfeld and Nicolson, 1981.

Wolynn, Mark. *It Didn't Start with You: How Inherited Family Trauma Shapes Who We Are and How to End the Cycle*. New York: Penguin Life, 2016.

Acknowledgements

This book took almost two decades to write. Maybe I'm a slow writer. Maybe it just took that long to process what it means to be motherless. In any case, taking my time allowed me to appreciate the blessings of generous people throughout my life and experiences that allowed me to become a person my mother would've been proud of. Far from perfect, I'm a woman satisfied with a lifetime of sustaining memories. I haven't reached the end of this particular journey on my own, however.

First, I'd like to thank Tara Neilson, who selected my manuscript from the many submissions to the Minerva Rising Press 2021 Memoir Contest. I'm both humbled and honored by her comments and by her confidence that my story was worth telling. I'm very grateful for Minerva Rising's talented and discerning nonfiction editor, Rebecca Beardsall, who suggested improvements and new insights at several points in the narrative. The book is much better because of her perceptiveness. Thanks also to all the staff—design, editing, and marketing—at

Minerva Rising Press for excelling at every step in the design and publication process. Minerva Rising Press is dedicated to empowering women to share their stories, and I'm proud to be among the authors they've chosen to publish.

I'd never have been able to write this book without a good foundation. Mary Cantrell, Teresa Miller, and Charlotte Gullick delivered expert instruction in storytelling arts over the years. Special thanks to Charlotte for detailed editing suggestions on an early draft of the book as well, what I refer to as "the amorphous vomitous mass." For getting me across the finish line, I'd like to thank Marion Roach Smith, whose Memoir Project Master Class made it possible to complete the first draft during early COVID-19 quarantine. I've taken many writing classes over the years and have had inspiring teachers and mentors, but Marion's professional guidance and no-nonsense instruction gave me the kick in the pants I needed to get it done.

Many thanks to my thoughtful and creative memoir writing cohorts, who took the Master Class with me and continued meeting over the next year and a half, while we shared chapters and revised manuscripts. Each of them encouraged, critiqued, and inspired; I couldn't have finished this book without them. Jan Hogle was there via email or Zoom to cheer me on when I was discouraged and to recommend resources to help with the next best step. Maria Olujic contributed on-point comments and constructive suggestions, whether she was at home in California or in her native Croatia. Thanks also to Alexandra Bush, who joined our little group from her expatriate life in Kosovo when she could.

For all those women—teachers, family members, church women, assorted mothers, and women friends—who provided living and loving examples of what a woman and mother could be, whether named within these pages or not, I'm deeply indebted. They'll never know the significance of their presence. I count myself truly fortunate to have shared my journey with three wonderful bonus sisters and the many wise and witty women friends who know me well but like me anyway! My life is so much richer because of them.

I want to thank my brother Jon and his wife Trudy for sharing memories with me, some of which made their way into the book. I'm blessed to have them both so near, where we can create fresh memories together, after too many years of living hundreds of miles apart. We all hoped to lure Karen here as well, but she didn't quite make it.

I want my children, Marc and Kelly, to know how proud I am of who they've become. It was a joy to watch them grow into creative, compassionate adults, and into the loving parents they are to my three fantastic grandchildren. Being their mother has been an honor! I'm also thankful for their splendid partners, Ruth and Dennis.

My husband, Tim, deserves my deepest love and respect. He's been my best friend for over fifty years and offered the encouragement I needed to complete this book, not to mention his patient listening to my whining when I couldn't seem to put my ideas into the right words. I'm not sure what I've done to deserve such a kind, smart, and faithful partner, but I'm profoundly grateful for the life we've shared. *W* to the max!

Janice Airhart takes seriously what her father once told her: "You can be anything you want to be." As a result, she's been a medical technologist, biomedical research tech, freelance writer and editor, science teacher to pregnant teens, bioscience program representative, and adjunct English professor. She now devotes her time to her first passion, writing that makes a difference, particularly in the lives of children and youth. An avid volunteer, Airhart reads with elementary children at an underperforming school, works with community nonprofits such as Jail to Jobs for youthful offenders, and participates in programs presented by the National Alliance on Mental Illness, Central Texas. Her essays and articles have appeared in *The Sun, The Science Teacher, Lutheran Woman Today, Story Circle Network's Real Women Write* 2019 and 2021 anthologies, and *One Woman's Day* blog. Her essay, "Migration" about the plight of displaced Afghan women and girls appeared in the Spring, 2022 issue of the *Concho River Review*. Devoted to encouraging women to tell their unique stories, she will present a session entitled "Journaling Your Story" at an upcoming Presbyterian women's gathering.

Airhart recently moved with her husband Tim, their dog Bella, and cat Ollie to Leander, Texas, a stone's throw from family in Austin and Round Rock.

www.ingramcontent.com/pod-product-compliance
Lightning Source LLC
Chambersburg PA
CBHW020922090426
42736CB00010B/1004

* 9 7 8 1 9 5 0 8 1 1 1 6 8 *